NATIVE WISDOM FOR WHITE MINDS

DAILY REFLECTIONS INSPIRED BY THE NATIVE PEOPLES OF THE WORLD

ANNE WILSON SCHAEF, PH.D.

ONE WORLD
BALLANTINE BOOKS • NEW YORK

A One World Book
Published by Ballantine Books

Copyright © 1995 by Anne Wilson Schaef

Owing to limitations of space, permission acknowledgments can be found on pp. 414–418, which constitute an extension of this copyright page.

An album of recorded music inspired by *Native Wisdom for White Minds* is available from Narada Records.

Library of Congress Cataloging-in-Publication Number: 94-96757

ISBN 0-345-39405-4

TEXT DESIGN BY DEBBY JAY

Manufactured in the United States of America
First Edition: August 1995
10 9 8 7 6 5 4 3

THIS BOOK IS DEDICATED TO

Kate and Frank Fools Crow
Auntie Helena Maka Santos
Auntie Elizabeth Beresford
Dame Whina Cooper
Uncle Henry Robinson

all of whom shared their love and wisdom while living on
this planet.

And to Native Elders, the world over, whose love and
guidance has brought this book into being.

The author will share a portion of her royalties
with Native people throughout the world
to help support individual
and group projects.

ACKNOWLEDGMENTS

This book is the work and sharing of many people and, most expressedly, a joint effort of Native and non-Native people throughout the world. There is no way to name all who have been involved, and I do want to acknowledge a few by name.

This book has come into being as a result of a mandate from Frank Fools Crow. Only as I began to work on it did I realize that Frank was working very closely with me, and that this was part of the work he had given me to do so many years ago. One has to grow into a name and vision. It took me some time, and I am grateful to know that Frank's work and mandate have been slumbering within me until I reached a time of readiness.

I want to thank the American Indian Science and Engineering Society for giving me a home, and Norbert Hill for recognizing that I needed one.

I would like to express my deep gratitude to the members of the American Indian Council of Elders for opening their hearts and meetings to me. I especially want to thank Phil and Bow Lane, whose "tepee flap is always open" to me and who have been my teachers, mentors, friends, and Elders. George and Peggy Goodstriker are also mentors as well as brother and sister to me, as is Lenore Stiffarm. Jeanette Timentwa is another mentor and friend, as are Horace and Andrea Axtell.

I want to thank Phil Lane, Jr., and the Four Worlds Project for their teachings, and the Earth Ambassadors Program for honoring me by making me an Elder to their program. Don Coyhis and Debra LaFontaine of White Bison, Inc., have given loving support and input, for which I am grateful.

Numerous Maori Marae have taken me in as family and shared their knowledge and wisdom with me. I want especially to thank the TE HA Maori program and Monica Takahanga at Saint Elizabeth's Hospital in New Zealand, and the Takahanga Marae in Kaikoura.

Mr. Reuben Kelly, Doreen, Kathy, and Brian, and Aunt Millie, Lorraine, and Hope have opened the Koorie world to me in Australia and brought soothing knowledge to my being. Cheryl Ahoy at the Koorie Keeping Place has been a sister.

Anne Elizabeth O'Malley has been an Irish friend and teacher for me, helping me to reach back into my Celtic roots.

Everlyn Nicodemus has been a longtime friend and mentor and has shared African truths of the soul with me. Her husband, Kristian Romare, has given me candid and brilliant support.

Marlene Helgamo has taken me back to Sun Dance and my people.

Anne, Angeline, and Auntie Margaret have given me the healing love of Lomi Lomi and cleansing to keep my body healthy. My Hawaiian friends and Kupuna Elders have loved and guided me.

Margaret Olk, Pete Sidley, Mike Church, Astrid Klein, and many others have helped gather material. My family, Roddy, and Beth, have been there for me throughout. Mary Ann Wells and Amie Nelson have offered needed support, and Ann Sprague has typed, followed up, loved, encouraged, and attended to details. Chuck has been there as companion and support in numerous sessions with Elders. I owe much to Betty Parent and Carolyn Miller and many others in my life who love and support me.

Jonathon Lazear, my agent, has added, "Yes, yes, good, good," throughout the process.

I can never completely express the joy and gratitude I feel for the pure pleasure of working with my editor, Cheryl Woodruff, her assistant, Leah Odze, and the wonderful team at Ballantine. There is no experience more cherished and treasured by an author than to have her work understood and supported for what it is. I have certainly had this experience at One World/Ballantine. I thank the Creator for all the help, support, and understanding.

Most of all, I want to thank my father, Paul, for giving me my Native heritage, and my mother, Manilla, for preserving that heritage deep within me.

INTRODUCTION

O Great Spirit, who made all races, look kindly upon the whole human family and take away the arrogance and hatred which separates us from our brothers.

—Cherokee Prayer

A prayer for our oneness. This position of oneness is where most Native peoples begin, and it is always done with prayer. Everything is done with prayer.

For the past several years I have spent large blocks of time with Native peoples and most especially Native Elders. Intuitively, I knew this was what my mind and my soul needed.

I came to write this book as a white mind struggling to heal and find freedom.

It was many years ago that the concept of a "white mind" came into my consciousness. The first time I remember thinking of the term *white mind* was when I had the honor of getting to know Frank and Kate Fools Crow. Frank Fools Crow was a great Ceremonial Chief and Spiritual Leader of the Lakota people. Frank Fools Crow became a very important person in my life, and his influence and impact on me have continued to grow long after his death. Some of the most powerful ceremonies I have ever experienced were with him.

After one ceremony that was of particular importance to me, he sat and talked with me. He told me that in his first vision quest, he had learned that he was to bring healing to the white people and he felt that he had failed. He then said that he was giving this responsibility to me. I remember thinking, *Of course you couldn't heal the white people, regardless of how powerful you are, because it takes a white mind to understand white minds. They're quirky.*

I then promptly forgot everything he'd said to me and anything I'd thought at the time—although occasionally the term *white mind* would resurface. Lately, though, when I've been sitting with Native people, the phrase *you white folks* often comes up. I began to see that this meant something more subtle than people of the white race. *You white folks* did mean white people, of course. However, I also began to realize that "you white people" was referring to the whole perspective of Western culture and to the white minds trained in and wedded to Western civilization.

Native people know that white minds see, conceptualize the world, and think differently than Native minds. As Herb Kawainui Kane says, "Primal cultures are essentially much alike, as proved by the universality of their myths; but worldviews, beliefs, and attitudes of primal societies are so fundamentally different from those of the modern Western society that what may be perfectly logical to one group may seem bizarre and incomprehensible to the other."

I have found what Herb Kane says to be true. Still, it is so difficult for white minds to really perceive these differences and appreciate them. This is because white minds are trained to believe that there is only one right answer, one right way of perceiving the world—and that singular way can only be mastered by minds trained in the Western scientific method of thinking. Unfortunately, Western culture's way of training our minds has resulted in closed-system thinking.

For example, in a closed system, white minds set up their world in dualisms. It's either this or that. Black or white. Right or wrong. This is a very limited and limiting way of thinking. In fact, I've found that the use of the word *but* usually sets up a dualism. For myself, I try to use *and* instead of *but* to help my mind break out of the dualistic form. I've tried to do this all through this book. Test it out for yourself. See what your mind does when you read an *and* where you think a *but* should be.

Why are we so afraid of acknowledging our white-mindedness? Why is there a seeming underlying shame in identifying ourselves as having a white mind? Why do we have such difficulty admitting we don't know and understand everything? Perhaps, part of the reason is that we've been taught that Western mechanistic science gives us the key to unlock the universe, and if there are realities for which this key does not work, those realities must simply be thought out of existence. This process of thinking that which is not understood out of existence is characteristic of a closed system. White minds, seemingly, only feel secure in a closed system.

White minds are often ruled by abstract intellectual constructs that get in the way of our accessing our universal minds or spirit. A white mind has been taught to break down its world into component parts in order to try to understand how things work. White minds reduce and isolate. They don't readily move into wholes or universality. They are hierarchical and mechanistic, and see nature as a force to be tamed and used up with no regard for the future. They cannot understand that they are a part of nature. They cannot see that nature is one with all of us—a gift to be valued and sustained. White minds often have to destroy to understand or to accept what is.

Let me say here that it's not only white people who have white minds. During the civil rights movement of the 1960s blacks often spoke of "Oreos"—people who are black on the outside and white on the inside. Native Americans speak of "apples"—red on the outside and white on the inside. In the South Pacific, it's "coconuts"—brown on the outside, white on the inside. We rarely hear these

3

terms today because Native peoples the world over are beginning to meet and share their wisdom with each other. White minds have difficulty reflecting upon themselves because they're trained to believe that the way they think is the only reality, and that they are the only reality. Yet, most of us have the capacity to transcend our white minds. We simply need help from outside ourselves to be able to move beyond our own limited views, and to reflect upon ourselves in a meaningful way.

Today, our white minds are proving destructive to ourselves and to our planet. Yet, growth, change, and healing are still possible. It means listening with open hearts and open minds to other voices, other perceptions, other cultures with which we share this earth of ours.

WARNING: THIS BOOK MAY BE HAZARDOUS TO YOUR ILLUSIONS!

What is being offered to us by the Native peoples in this book is not just another form of political correctness. Being wedded to appearances is so characteristic of Western culture. So many of us want to get an intellectual idea of change and not really change the way we see and the way we live our lives every day. What we're being offered is the opportunity to move from white minds to global minds. We're being offered the possibility of moving out of the cave of white-mindedness into the waters of planetary wisdom.

So often, I've heard Elders from a wide variety of Native people say, "Our legends and myths have told us that a time would come when it would be necessary for us to share our wisdom and knowledge, and that time is now. They say, "Our legends tell us that a time will come when our wisdom and way of living will be necessary to save the planet and now we have decided to speak."

This is an impressive message—and all the more remarkable that this same message is coming from so many diverse peoples the world over. I find it incredible that these people are willing to share with anyone who will truly listen—even if the listener comes from a culture that has tried to annihilate them. Their concern is much broader than societal grudges, customs, or politics. Eddie Box, a much revered Ute Elder and medicine man, shared with me what one of his Elders had told him: "And he said when you get rid of that anger and resentment toward whites for what they have done, everything you ask with His name [the Creator] will come to you—no difficulty. Because you have built a compassion inside of you to the human race of the world. See, that is what they [the old Elders] were talking about."

So, now that we know that white minds aren't bad minds— they're just one way of trying to be human, are you ready for *Native Wisdom for White Minds*? This is a book that dares you to be un-comfortable. It offers you the opportunity to grow beyond the lim-itations of our most cherished illusions. It asks you to participate in conceptual blockbusting. It offers you reintegration at a soul level.

If you're ready to move from only experiencing life at a personal level to experiencing life at a universal level, this book is for you. It's a book for people who want to explore, create, and confront their isolation and loneliness of the soul. A book for people who are willing to trek in the desert of their separation so that they can move into feelings of connectedness and oneness at a level they may never have felt before.

As you sit with this book day by day, you may find your white mind expanding into unknown territory, as I did. This book can support the process of your shifting into a different way of being in the world. It offers you nothing less than a spiritual revolution—a revolution of mind, a total transformation of worldview. I have personally taken the journey I am now inviting you to begin. Over the years, I have sat with Native Elders and been welcomed into the homes and lives of Native people the world over. Just being with them has enriched my life so much. As I began to experience spiritual and emotional healing that I could never have imagined before, I realized that I needed to share this wisdom with as many other people as possible.

I want to make clear that I have had no need to delve into secrets that Native people are not willing to share. I do not need to know their secrets—their rituals, their ceremonies, or their hidden ways of healing. While I have had the honor of participating in some of their ceremonies and rituals, my experience in many of them is much too private and personal to share.

White minds tend to seek out ceremonies, rituals, or magic as a "fix." They don't seem to understand that they cannot use these "secrets" in some mechanistic way. For when this knowledge is not deeply grounded in the worldview of its own culture, it loses all meaning and power. To experience this larger, more inclusive worldview takes time, and patience, and participation. It cannot be learned as an intellectual exercise.

LIKE WATER ON SANDSTONE

I am aware that there is a fascination with books about indigenous peoples, especially Native Americans. Yet these books are often read and then just put away. This is not a book about the "noble savage" or the romanticizing of Native people. Most of the people with whom I have sat are just "regular" people. They have made mistakes, been warlike, left their spirituality at times, and displayed their humanness. We cannot dismiss them as being perfect or imperfect. They are simply people.

Yet they bring us a great gift. For what they have to teach us is another worldview. And they don't have to be perfect human beings to do that. Nor do we have to dismiss what they're saying because we find imperfections in their teachings—that's simply another white-mind trick!

When I thought about how to present this material, I decided to write it in the form of a meditation book. I've had some success with this form, and I like the idea of taking a bit of time each day to sit with these ideas, this healing, this worldview. Because changing worldviews takes time, I wanted the experience of this wisdom to seep in like water on sandstone—a slow process that leaves its mark.

I didn't expect this book to fit the usual concept of a meditation book—to be soothing and healing. I don't believe that being soothing and/or giving directions or answers is necessarily healing. I believe that real healing takes place at a deep level and often requires some painful cleansing along the way. This takes time and cannot be simplified.

All of the Native people quoted in this book have experienced violence and genocide from white people and Western culture, and yet their message to us is one of deep concern, peace, and healing—healing for us as individuals, healing for our societies, and healing for our planet.

THIS WISDOM IS FOR LIVING

Although *Native Wisdom for White Minds* is presented in the form of a meditation book, it is much more than that. It is historical, educational, political, and informational. It is confrontive, healing, provocative, expanding, loving, comforting, hopeful, and above all spiritual. Jesus said, "You shall know the truth and the truth shall set you free." There is freedom in this wisdom—freedom because it helps us return to our deep inner knowing. We may have forgotten this wisdom and I do not believe it is gone. The knowledge and wisdom of ancient ways has simply been slumbering in our souls, awaiting a time to be reawakened. The Elders believe that time is now, and I trust their wisdom. Without their help and guidance this book could not have been written. The message is theirs. I am only the messenger.

Each entry in this book presents a place for Native people to offer a voice as they want to speak. I have not tampered with their

7

voices. Rarely do we have the opportunity to hear Native voices not modified for white ears. Then, after each person has spoken, I have shared my responses and what I have learned.

Only as we broaden our base and are willing, truly, to learn from the diversity around us can we begin to see that we have confused culture with nature. We have confused *our* culture with reality. As Helena Norberg-Hodge writes in *Ancient Futures*, "I had not realized that many of the negative trends I saw were the result of my own industrial culture rather than some natural, evolutionary force beyond our control."

I agree with her as she goes on to say, "Our static and mechanistic worldview has reached its limits, and some scientists—particularly quantum physicists—now speak of a paradigm shift away from the old 'building block' view of reality to a more organic one. In direct opposition to the trend in mainstream culture toward greater specialization, we need to actively promote the generalists—the one who sees connection and makes links across different disciplines. In this regard, one of the most hopeful trends is the increasing respect for more feminine values and ways of thinking." And, I might add, more respect for Native values.

Over the years, part of Frank Fools Crow's ceremonies and his words have come back to me—always at the right time. As I began working on this book, I suddenly remembered his passing along to me the responsibility of bringing healing to white people. It was a powerful incentive for me to continue writing, and I felt I had his blessing.

I also remember what happened the first time I met with Australian Aboriginal Elders. They greeted me and then said, "Why are you here?"

I didn't know. I just "knew" I was supposed to be there, and they had, after all, invited me. Others tried to speak on my behalf and say the right things.

I knew better deep in my soul, so I finally said, "I'm here to see why I'm here."

8

They liked that and said, "Well, yes, but what took you so long? You were supposed to be here four years ago." I was! And it had not worked out.

"Then you were supposed to be here two years ago." I *was*, and instead had an emergency appendectomy!

"Well, you're here now, so let's get on with it." And they promptly started talking among themselves and ignored me, teaching me a great deal.

I've had the feeling and have been informed that Native people the world over are choosing people with whom to share their message. Most of these people are Native, and some are not. I have prayed about this responsibility, sought council from the Elders and from Native groups, and begged for guidance. It is the Native way to teach what can be taught and then to trust you. This isn't "my" book, and I *do* take responsibility for it.

With the exception of the entries about Ladakh, all of the material in this book comes from cultures with which I have had personal contact, including writings and literature. I have not been able to include all tribal cultures, and that, I feel, is my and our loss. Nor have I included information from anthropologists. In my experience, most of their material has been interpreted from a Western cultural perspective and is thus not representative of what the people themselves are saying. Also most tribal people I've met do not trust anthropologists, which is reason enough to leave their words out.

The wisdom in this book is for living . . . for living with. Native cultures have much to teach us. They know how to live in balance with themselves, with each other, with nature, and with the earth. There is an inner balance that emerges that invites us into aliveness, joy, and peace as a way of living our lives, not just as some abstract concept. I offer this wisdom to you. I only hope that, with my "white mind," I have presented this wisdom in a way that is both respectful to the Elders and their knowledge and useful to you.

I was born near the Cherokee Nation, and my mother was more Indian than white. I am so grateful to her for all she taught me. Many years ago a Native American medicine man said to me, "You use a lot of Indian medicine in your work. You know more than you use. And when you are ready, come to me and I will teach you what you need to know."

I have never gone to spend time with him, and yet I have been called to spend more and more time with Native peoples. I have needed to do this for my healing and for my sanity. Since I was raised among Native people and my mother was an Indian in her soul, in her way of being, and in her way of living, I came out of a philosophy of life that is community based, one with nature, and spiritual. Having been well trained in academia, I did not know the depth of my Native roots—but that old medicine man did. That was almost twenty years ago. I can now see that what I'm teaching and calling the Living Process System (living in a new paradigm) is based on a Native worldview.

I make no claim to having a real grasp of Native wisdom the way Native people do, since I was raised a white person. Yet I feel very comfortable sharing how it has affected me, what I've learned from it, and how my work emerges out of it. I know that my time with the Elders and Native people was what I needed for myself. I know that what I've discovered in myself because of this is only the tip of the iceberg. Most of all, I know that this wisdom and this worldview are important for us all now. I am no longer comfortable with Western ways of healing, especially with a psychology that is based on a mechanistic scientific worldview.

One week after I submitted the manuscript, I was at a family reunion, and my aunt casually said over her shoulder, "You knew your father was an American Indian, didn't you?"

"No," I said. "Was he?"

"I'm surprised your mother didn't tell you. He was. I'm sure of it. Cherokee, I believe."

My white mind had found its Native soul and a new journey had begun.

JANUARY

FROM OLD TO OLD TO NEW

The oft-quoted *whakatauki* states, *Ka pu te ruha, ka hao te rangatahi*—as the old net piles up on shore, the new net goes fishing. The tauira [pattern, or model] of the old provides the basis of formation for the new. The new time dictates changes in both the structure and form of the new net, and also in the choice of fishing ground. By casting it to sea, the old net may tell us even more than we dare hope for. The care taken is reassuring. It is the fishing exercise that now commands our attention, and this must be executed in the same spirit in which the old net was prepared and made.

—*Piri Sciascia,* Maori Writer

We are in a time of changing nets. The old scientific world paradigm is thrashing, groaning, and lashing out as we hear the constant message "This hasn't worked. It's time to change."

It is time that we return to the knowledge and wisdom of the old net—ancient Native cultures and the wisdom of our Elders—while recognizing that "the new time dictates changes in both the structure and form of the new net" as well as in the "choice of fishing ground."

As we have become more and more willing to cast the old into the sea, we must take care to recognize that a time of change requires that we be present, that we learn from our past, that we do not cling to a "known" that is not working. We need the courage to make new nets and cast them onto new fishing grounds.

@

Native people's wisdom helps me move into a new way of being on this planet.

DIVINITY

If grains of sand can become a reflection of the divine, just think what can happen to the human being.

—*His Holiness the Dalai Lama,* Tibet

Sometimes we forget our potential. We become so wrapped up in the muckiness of living day to day that we become like eagles whose talons are stuck in tar.

Each new day brings us the opportunity to remember that every one of us is a reflection of the divine. Our inner beings know this— they never forget. Unfortunately, we live in a society that does its best to help us forget our most basic inner knowing. We need to remember, not dismember, our divine.

Our reflection of the divine is ever present. With our divinity comes responsibility. When I remember this, everything is possible.

POSSESSIVENESS

You don't need to ask me permission to quote something I have written or said. We are both doing the work of the Creator. Our responsibility is to get the information out there. Use whatever you like.

—*Don Coyhis*
Mohican Writer and Consultant
American Indian

This was the answer given to me by Don Coyhis, president of the White Bison Society, when I asked him if I might use some words from his wonderful new meditation book based on the Medicine Wheel and Native American spirituality.

There are some Native people who feel that they have been exploited enough and they're not willing to share with white people anymore, and I understand their position. Then there are people like Don.

Most Native people I know are like Don. They realize that possession—of anything, and especially of words—is an illusion. Once we put them out there, they belong to the universe. If we are all, to the best of our ability, doing the work of the Creator, there is no possession.

I assured Don that I felt the same way about his using my material. Our interaction felt so sane, so truly human.

When I am doing the work of the Creator, possession is an illusion.

NATIVE WISDOM

It was a Hawaii where birds, clouds, and stones spoke as clearly as people, because the silent language of nature was profoundly understood.

—*Nana Veary*, Hawaiian Kupuna

We live in a world that is filled with the possibility of conversation. The language of nature is as varied and complex as the many human languages that exist. There is nothing as impressive as being with an old Hawaiian Elder while she "reads" nature.

We Westerners are full of questions: What did it say? What does it mean? How do you know? Our mechanistic science has taken it upon itself to understand and then to control nature.

Hawaiian people have no need to control nature or even to understand it . . . rationally. Conversing with nature, hearing the stones talk, listening to the bird messengers, and reading the sea are all possibilities when we are one with nature.

We all understand our own Native language best, regardless of how many others we learn. And our true Native language is nature. As we allow ourselves to become one with it, we experience a level of profundity that cannot be communicated in human terms.

❧

It takes a lot of listening to hear what the rocks are saying.

FEAR

"Why do they whisper; why are they so afraid?" [said of the *Paheka*, White people]

—*Witi Ihimaera*, Maori Writer

Whispers, secrets, mumblings. . . . In Western culture, we seem to believe that God hates our speaking out. We are always told to whisper and be quiet in "sacred" places. But—there is more to it. Native people the world over have observed that white Westerners seem to be afraid.

What are we so afraid of? Are we afraid of others? Maybe. Are we afraid of ourselves? Maybe. Are we afraid of the Creator, of our Higher Power, of God? Maybe.

Fear is generated by estrangement. When we no longer experience ourselves as a participating part of the universe, when we lose our sense that we're a part of a universal community that needs us just as much as we need it, when we pull ourselves out of the awareness of the oneness of all things, we feel afraid.

It is difficult for Native people to understand that alienation, unless they have adopted Western culture.

❀

My fear is my indicator that something is wrong. It is the Creator's way of saying, "Come on back."

❖❖❖❖❖❖❖❖❖❖❖❖❖❖❖❖❖❖

FAMILY/CHILDREN

You white people don't understand what we mean by "family." When a baby is born, it is given to its "mother." That means, the mother who bore it, all her sisters and all her aunties. They are responsible for caring for it and teaching it. It is also given to all its "fathers." That means, its natural father, all his brothers and all his uncles. They are responsible for caring for it and teaching it. Everyone else in the tribe is brother and sister.

We think it is really primitive for a baby to have only one mother and one father!

—Australian Aboriginal Elder

Many children, in Western society, don't even have two parents!

Imagine the love, support, and caring we would experience with a whole group of mothers and fathers! Imagine what that would do to our modern psychological views that a baby has to "bond" with a mother and that if this does not occur, the child will be incomplete and unable to cope with society and life.

Imagine what would happen if we viewed ourselves as having infinite possibilities for intimacy. Imagine being able to avail ourselves of the security that a whole cadre of parents could offer us! The options for relatedness that tribal connections offer have yet to be tapped in Western culture, and sadly, we keep moving farther and farther from the possibilities.

☯

Are we, indeed, "primitive" in our assumptions that two parents are enough for one child? Maybe "existential angst" is only a part of Western culture—not necessarily a given of the human condition.

‣◆‣◆‣◆‣◆‣◆‣◆‣◆‣◆‣◆‣◆‣◆‣◆‣◆‣◆‣◆‣◆‣◆‣

SPIRITUAL HELP

Those that fail—with our brothers and sisters—they need our spiritual help. Pray for them.

—*Annie Cotton,* Blood Tribe Elder
Canada

Sound familiar? Pray for your enemies. We hear this in all of the world's religions. We hear this in Twelve Step programs. Yet, it does not seem to have become an integral part of Western culture.

Imagine a whole way of life where when someone—anyone—falls down, or does wrong, or is bad in word and deed, everyone prays for that person. How simple! How simple to realize that we have spiritual help to give and that others need it! How powerful and clear (and yes, even humble) we feel when we know that being a spiritual being is a natural state for us and we have spiritual help to offer.

෨෧

When I know I have spiritual help to give, it is easy to "pray for them."

SHARING/GIVING AWAY

I am a big man. See all these shells? They are very valuable in our culture. I could have trunks of them . . . but then I wouldn't be a big man. A big man gives away what he has and shares with others.

—New Guinea Elder

In almost all Native cultures, to accumulate, hold on to, hoard, or have much more than you need is an embarrassment. What if we all lived in a world where each person, each animal, each element, took only what it needed and no more?

Yet, Western mechanistic science is based on the belief that the only things that are real or of value are those we can register with our senses or with mechanical extensions of the senses such as microscopes, and so forth. This emphasis on empirical proof has resulted in measuring, counting, and controlling.

All spiritual paths tell us to believe in and hold to the unseen, not the seen.

Native cultures are showing us a way to shift our perceptions so that we can focus our attention on and value the unseen. We now have a chance to become the spiritual beings that we were created to be and thus learn to live in greater harmony with this material world. We can now discover what sharing is all about.

❧

I have so often given myself *away that somehow I've become confused about the meaning of sharing and giveaways.*

<⊙><⊙><⊙><⊙><⊙><⊙><⊙><⊙><⊙><⊙><⊙><⊙><⊙><⊙><⊙><⊙><⊙>

INTERCONNECTEDNESS

The honor of one is the honor of all. The hurt of one is the hurt of all.

> —*Phil Lane, Jr.*, Yankton Sioux/Chickasaw
> Four Worlds Institute
> American Indian

When one is honored, we all benefit. There is no real competition except with ourselves. When we are following our own path and being respectful of that path, we hope and assume that others are doing the same. Therefore, when others accomplish something and are honored for that accomplishment, it is because they have been true to their path. Since all of us are connected and are sisters and brothers, we feel proud when members of our human family are honored.

As a part of this creation, we are interconnected with everything. When any part of this creation is violated or wounded, we feel that violation. We are *affected* by that violation. Since we are all participants in this great creation, we hurt when others are hurt. Wounding is not individual.

🌀

In sharing the honor and the hurt of all, I have the possibility of becoming one with all Creation. I can, therefore, move beyond what I, by myself, can be and do.

DIFFERENCES

A fact which is often ignored is that women who know well and accept their positions in their own society, willingly carry out their family duties and other demands and obligations relating to their community. They are recognised and admired for their efforts. They are respected for displaying specific female qualities in accordance with the values and beliefs of the people and are greatly appreciated for playing the roles appropriate to their defined positions within the family or community hierarchy. It is only when one is aspiring to a different way of life made possible by the presence of alternative life-styles and the freedom of choice, that one begins to make a low evaluation of the position and contribution of women in Fijian communities; and to unfairly compare two different life-styles which could only be meaningfully understood and appreciated in their respective contexts.

—*Asesela Ravuvu,* Fijian Writer

One of the diseases of the Western mind has been to place ourselves at the center of the universe. We have arrogantly assumed that our way is better when we have not experienced, known, and/or participated in other ways of living. Like an amoeba, we send our egos out on false feet, or "pseudopods," to attempt to bring anything different into our culture—our food vacuole—in order to absorb it into ourselves or reject it, spit it out, destroy it.

Native people respect the essence of the other.

෴

Today, I have a chance to see and respect differences.

WHOLENESS/AWARENESS

Modern ecology can learn a great deal from a people who managed and maintained their world so well for 50,000 years.
> —*Burnum Burnum*
> Australian Aboriginal Writer

How do we "live with" the land? What do we need to learn in order to develop an awareness that we are dependent upon the earth for our very existence? Reverence cannot evolve from an attitude of raping, exploiting, and using up.

How do we find our proper place on this planet? Saving aluminum cans may make us feel better, and it is doing *something*. Yet, what we really need is to shift our focus from one of dominance to once of reverence and participation. We need to realize that we are humans participating in a living universe where we are only one part of a huge cast of characters that includes everything around us—the seen and the unseen.

It takes the pressure off to see that we are only a part of an evolving whole.

HUMOR

"Yer man's" . . . wit is generally the good-humoured kind saying "serious things in a way that seem funny when you see how serious they are."

—*Sean McCann,* Irish Writer

Humor is the ability to make light of something that is deadly serious, thereby taking the "deadly" out of it and putting the life back into it.

A society that is humorless is a lifeless society. When things become so serious—and so sacred—that we can't laugh about them anymore, it means we have elevated the profane to the realm of the sacred and misplaced the sacred in the process.

❀

There's nothing funnier than an addict who thinks he isn't.

COMPARISON

She [the author] learnt from her Elders that everything in the universe is perfect. People and anything else only become less than perfect when compared to someone or something else, or when influenced by negative forces.

—*Rangimarie Turuki Pere*, Maori Writer

In Western culture we are taught to understand ourselves and our world by comparison, contrast, dualism, and similarity. It is difficult for us even to imagine that the way other people think and the thinking processes themselves differ from our own.

Imagine the shock of discovering that the majority of people in the world do not use the same *thinking processes* that we do! In fact, in some circles, the use of comparison, contrast, dualism, and similar forms of thinking are linked with schizophrenia and addictive thinking processes.

If everything in the universe is perfect, I don't need to compare myself or anything to anyone or anything else. I'm learning to accept people and things as they are. The way I have been taught to think affects me more than I realize.

THE PRACTICAL

Always remove your shoes before entering a local house.
—*Ann Kondo Corum,* Hawaiian Writer

Everyone takes their shoes off first. I don't know why. I could come up with a lot of reasons: Less dirt . . . no hard-to-clean red clay in the house . . . respect . . . because that's the way you do it . . . saves the carpets . . . saves the floors . . . you don't want the energy from the outdoors carried into the house.

All I really know is that it is a *custom* in Hawaii to remove your shoes before entering a house. So we all do it.

Besides, I like padding around in bare feet. I like slipping into "house slippers" when I enter, not having to clean as much, having that time for other things. I like shedding the outside world when I enter "my place" or "someone else's place." I like having people respect my home and my time. I like taking my shoes off when I enter a house.

❧

Sometimes, what we learn from other cultures doesn't have to be political or spiritual. It can just be something good to do.

LISTENING/WISDOM

You white folk—you're always asking questions. You never just watch and listen. You can usually learn what you need to know by watching and listening.

—Native American Elder

Think for a moment about the tyranny of the questions "Why is this?" "What is that?" "What's the explanation?" "Can you prove it?"

When we view ourselves and our world as machines, we become deluded by the notion that if we just pick things apart—including ourselves—and understand how it all works, we will know . . . we will have wisdom.

Because of our thorough conviction that Western mechanistic science is the only avenue to reality and truth, we believe that information has to be received and processed rationally and logically and we want to feed it directly into our "computerized," logical left-brain function.

We have lost the ability to watch and listen. We have lost the ability to notice. We have lost the ability to let information process us. We have lost the avenue to wisdom when we accept the belief that the only true knowledge is that which can be processed logically and rationally.

Native people have always known that spirituality and a relationship with the Great Spirit require a good deal of patient waiting and listening.

❧

When I can watch my questions pass through my mind like clouds across a summer sky, I have stepped upon the path to wisdom.

PRAYER

Kia hora te marino, kia whakapapa pounamu te moana, kia tere ai te karohirohi i mua tonu i o koutou huarahi.

May the calm be widespread, may the sea be as the smooth surface of the greenstone, and may the rays of sunshine forever dance along your pathway.

—Maori Prayer

A Maori prayer—how much of Maori life is a prayer. Prayer, in the old Maori tradition, is as ever present as breathing. In fact, breathing is a form of prayer.

Also, peace is a reality in many Native cultures throughout the world. Peace is not a concept, it is the way the Creator expects us to live. When I am not living peacefully among others, I must look to myself to see why I am out of harmony, because harmony is the natural order.

Prayer is one way I become "right" with myself, others, and the planet. As I pray for you—whoever you are—I become right with myself.

❧

Kia tere ai te karohirohi i mua tonu i o koutou huarahi. *May the light forever dance across your path.*

SHAME

You don't ever have to be ashamed of who you are.
>—Spoken to Margaret Olk by *Peter John*
> Athabaskan Elder and Chief
> Minto, Alaska

I am enough! No matter what, the Creator created me and the Creator does not make mistakes. People make lots of mistakes. And, when we come to believe in the true meaning of being who we are, we understand that in being who we are, we fill a very necessary place in the universe. A place that does not fit for anyone else. To be ashamed of what the Creator has made is to insult the Creator.

I cannot insult myself without insulting the Creator. I cannot insult the Creator without insulting myself. I might as well accept that I'm enough!

SERENITY/ACCUMULATION/ONENESS

> The Christianity of the Celts—having no towns, no currency, no large-scale industries—had little temptation to material and worldly ideals. It retained a serene inner life.
>
> —*N. Chadwick,* Irish Writer

Again and again we experience the clash between a serene inner life and all the "things" of modern life. Is true spirituality dependent upon our giving everything away? Jesus certainly recommended it! Do we really have to be poor to be true in spirit? A mechanistic scientific worldview would certainly interpret this wisdom that way—do this to fix that—just like a car.

I think the issue is more complex. It's not really "things" we're talking about here. We're talking about the spirit with which we are living our lives on this planet. If our spirit is one of oneness and sharing, we don't need so much. If our spirit is one of knowing that we will get what we truly need, we don't need so much. If our spirit is one of respecting the earth and taking very little from her, we don't need so much.

☯

The issue is not one of giving things up. It's about coming into the serenity of our oneness with all things and participating in our universe. Then we don't need so much.

GOING EASY

Easy, easy—just go easy and you'll finish.

—Hawaiian Kupuna

Does this mean that it's okay to be lazy? Does this mean we don't have to work? Does it mean to stop the things we are doing? Maybe. Maybe not.

We have become so work addicted in Western culture, we find it incomprehensible that we will actually finish if we go easy.

A group of us have bought an old hot-springs hotel in Montana. We see ourselves as temporary custodians of a sacred healing place. When we bought it, the buildings were almost feeling the bull-dozer's blade. At first we were overwhelmed with what needed to be done. Then we decided to move slowly, to only do as much as we were able, one step at a time, sanely. This year, at the owners' meeting, we were astounded by how much had been accomplished, and we could scarcely believe it had been done in only three years.

When I go easy, I get more done.

WISDOM

Sr. Emilio Castro lived down a small foot path from my home. Every day he carried an unbelievable amount of building supplies on his back as he went to construct a small cottage on the mountainside. Or I would see him equally laden as he set off to the *milpa* [the corn field]. He was a very gentle man. One of those "illiterates" who spoke Spanish as well as Katchiquel and another Mayan dialect, a smattering of English too.

> —As told by *Latifa Amdur*, L.Ac., Dipl. Ac., and C.H.
> Guatemala

"Illiterate." What does that mean? How often we have used that word to describe people who are not like us. When we do this, we miss so much wisdom.

It is not only those formally educated in Western science and culture who are the brilliant teachers of this world. In fact, it is often those who have lived, experienced, known, and listened who possess the wisdom.

Knowledge can be learned. Wisdom must be lived.

❧

Wisdom is the process of living unfolding. It often waits for us where we least expect it.

POWER/HUMILITY

Aliye juu ni juu.

Wait below for he who is above. (He will fall.)

—Swahili Proverb

A person who climbs one-up also faces the possibility of going one-down. In fact, people who think in terms of being one-up tend to be caught in the dualism of one-up and one-down.

In most Native cultures around the globe, the people who are the leaders are often the most humble people around. They are not self-effacing. They are humble.

These leaders know deep within themselves that whatever power they have comes to them from the Creator and that it is a gift that comes laden with responsibility.

To live true power is possible only with great humility.

BEING PRESENT

While we were working we used to have meetings once a week. I used to tell them about work. I'd say, you have to have your mind on what you're doing at all times until you finish a job or you will get hurt. Carelessness is what hurts people. Makes accidents. As long as you're working at something that is real dangerous any time you go think about something else you sure will get hurt. You can move any heavy object like house or warehouse or fish wheel, but you got to have your mind on it.

—*Goodwin Semaken, Sr.,* Eskimo/Indian Elder
Yukon Territory, Alaska

Attention, presence, and noticing are all a part of living in the present. How often we try to do things with half a mind or half a heart! How often we believe that only a piece of us should suffice. We attempt to have intimate relationships in form only, and not in presence.

When we are not present to our situation, we set ourselves up to be injured, whether physically, emotionally, socially, or spiritually. Spiritual injury is progressive. It may not show as much as physical injury, and it is cumulative.

❧

My lack of presence is an insult to those I love. Including myself.

PARTICIPATION

Those who build the house are built by it.

—Maori Elder

How often we forget that the very task we are doing may have more effect upon us than we have upon it. In our self-centeredness, we see ourselves acting upon our world and we lose the awareness that we are participating in a universe that is acting in partnership *with* us. What a burden we put on ourselves when we see ourselves as the only or the primary actor.

It is through participation—through acting with—that we learn that the house builds itself. That as we build it, we are built by it in return. When we open ourselves to be taught what the house can teach us, we are open to invaluable learning.

☙

Only when I participate in the fullness around me can I learn from the fullness around me.

TEARS/BODY

The body is full of stuffed tears. Tears of grief and tears of rage and the steam makes the body cry. Then the body is ready to receive love.

—*Angeline Locey,* Hawaiian Healer and Kupuna

Many Native cultures include steam baths as part of the natural healing process and ongoing care of the body.

We store so much in the body. We eat too much, and we put in foods that are too fat, too sweet, too artificial, and we expect the body to receive all of this with no help. We put in feelings and emotions that we don't know how to process, or that we've forgotten how or refuse to, process. Slowly, the body becomes "stuffed" with "tears."

We need to give the body the opportunity to cleanse itself. We need to rid ourselves of stored-up grief and rage so that we have the opportunity to receive what is there for us.

@@

When I confuse being stuffed with being contented, I have some learning to do. I can start by letting my body cleanse itself.

STEWARDSHIP

Alina embwa: tasuula ggumba.

One who has a dog: does not throw away bones.
—Ugandan Proverb

Right! Don't throw away things that are useful. In Western culture, we're considered eccentric when we continue to use something that is outdated. Usefulness is no longer our criterion for longevity. And . . . how limited our concept of what is useful has become! We haven't even given ourselves the luxury of using our imaginations to find out what is useful.

It's not just materialism or consumerism that's our problem. These are just symptoms. The real problem is that we have come to value only that which is material and, in so doing, have run the risk of forfeiting our souls. *And*, we no longer see any value in taking time to use our imagination and creativity.

It is difficult to use what we have when we don't have the time to imagine usefulness. Unfortunately, we've put ourselves in the same position as the things around us. Sadly, much too often, we treat ourselves and others as throwaways.

๏๏

When we use what we already have, we don't need so much.

◄○►◄○►◄○►◄○►◄○►◄○►◄○►◄○►◄○►◄○►◄○►◄○►◄○►◄○►◄○►◄○►◄○►

CONTENTED IDLENESS

Contented idleness . . . was the succulent mistress of creativity.
—*Albert Wendt,* Samoan Writer

Ah, contented idleness! Time—time to sit—to watch—to think—to *not* think! How rare! How beautiful! It is only in the stopping, in the stillness, that we hear what is already there.

Some time ago, I was involved in what seemed a life-and-death struggle with my publisher about a book title. In trying to solve it, I got nowhere. Finding no solutions, I undressed and eased myself into the healing waters of an old Indian hot spring and floated—mindless. In no time, a possible solution came to me.

I am sure that this creative new idea would not have emerged if I had continued to think about it. I succumbed to "contented idleness."

&

We have much to learn about "contented idleness." Many of us will never have to cope with our creativity because we have not given ourselves the opportunity to embrace a life with "time held in suspension."

DIFFERENCES/UNIQUENESS

There are indigenous belief systems. In areas where sorcery is strong, it is women who hold spiritual power. Christianity has arrived with all its variations. But the spirit world has been part of our culture for generations.

—*Margaret Taylor*, Papua New Guinea Writer

When we value the unique talents of both men and women, we see that the entire range is not only necessary for a fully functioning society but that the variations enhance the society as a whole. Many Native cultures contain significant cultural roles for men who are more like women and for women who are more like men. When a culture assumes that each person is a gift from and a creation of the Creator, it's not so important that everyone be alike.

My spiritual power was created to serve all of Creation. I need to learn how to honor it.

TRUST/RECEPTION

The Australian Aboriginals do not have an abundance of food, yet, they eat "what presents itself to them" in an attitude of trust and reception.

—Westerner observing the practices of Australian Aboriginals

To live a life of faith in our daily existence is a great challenge. We set up a dualism of work: either labor to get what you need or don't work and starve. Either way we lose, and the dualism serves to keep us stuck because neither end is that enticing.

We are so bound up in our agendas and our plans that we have little time even to notice "what presents itself to us." We often miss what life is unfolding for us.

❧

If I start with living with only what I need, I will have the opportunity to live my life in an attitude of trust and receptivity.

LIVING IN THE PRESENT

His people lived in the present. . . . Their tempers would explode and they would send one another to the hospital with stone or machete or fist wounds. Then deep remorse, and all was forgiven.
—*Albert Wendt,* Samoan Writer

Living in the present. What does that really mean? Can forgiveness be so instantaneous a process that we no longer have the time, the energy, or the need to carry around old resentments, hatreds, or griefs?

Can life, indeed, be so precious that we want to be so fully present to each moment that we are no longer willing to enslave ourselves to the past?

We can learn from the past and then . . . let it go. To carry it with us prevents us from knowing our present and seeing what is there for us.

☺

Every great spiritual teacher has taught the need to be present in the moment. Yet, we must create a lifestyle and a cultural system that supports this possibility.

‹◊›‹◊›‹◊›‹◊›‹◊›‹◊›‹◊›‹◊›‹◊›‹◊›‹◊›‹◊›‹◊›‹◊›‹◊›‹◊›

FEELINGS/KNOWING/TRUST

The senses are contradictory and deceiving. We never look at anything with our senses. We look with our feelings. Only our feelings can be trusted.

—*Alex Pua,* Hawaiian Kupuna

Now there's a unique idea for Western minds! *Only our feelings can be trusted.*

We have built an entire civilization—and I use the term carefully—upon a belief that the logical and rational mind is the source of all truth and reality. What do we have to learn from a culture that says that our senses (on which the *science* of our own culture is based) are "contradictory and deceiving"?

In the Living Process System, I have long suggested that there is nothing wrong with our minds; it is just the order in which we use them. In Western culture, we take in information through our senses, we process it in the logical, rational half of the brain and let it tell us how we should feel about it.

In most other cultures of the world, and especially among the Hawaiian people, people take in information with their being, process it in the body, in the solar plexus, experienced as feelings, then they bring it up to the intuitive brain for more processing. Finally, they send it to the rational mind for words, concepts, and language.

When I trust my feelings, I am usually right.

◄○►◄○►◄○►◄○►◄○►◄○►◄○►◄○►◄○►◄○►◄○►◄○►◄○►◄○►◄○►◄○►

GRATITUDE

Let us give thanks for this beautiful day. Let us give thanks for this life. Let us give thanks for the water without which life would not be possible. Let us give thanks for Grandmother Earth who protects and nourishes us.

—Daily Prayer of the Lakota American Indian

To tribal people, every day is beautiful because it is a gift from the Creator. When we live in relationship with nature, we inherently know that the change of seasons and all kinds of weather are necessary for our continuation and that of the planet.

Only in Western culture, which is based upon judgment, perfectionism, and the illusion of control, have we come to believe that we should be able to control nature and that some days are better than others. We forget that we did not create this life we are living. It is a gift from the Creator, and we have the possibility—*the possibility*—of living it.

The earth sustains us. I recently heard a CEO of a major corporation, while praising science and technology, say to a group of American Indians, "Nature will not feed you." His ignorance was so blatant that no one felt any wish to correct him. However much we pillage and pollute Her, Grandmother Earth still feeds us. We cannot afford to poison our earth.

֍

Starting our day by giving thanks for the obvious that has become obscure to us may save us and the planet.

FEBRUARY

◄◇►◄◇►◄◇►◄◇►◄◇►◄◇►◄◇►◄◇►◄◇►◄◇►◄◇►◄◇►◄◇►◄◇►◄◇►◄◇►◄◇►

REVERENCE

We see God in Water, Sun, Air—everywhere.
> —*George Goodstriker,* Kainai (Blackfoot) Elder
> Canada

How luxurious! God is everywhere. How much more we could learn about God if we were open to the knowledge that pours into us every minute!

What beauty there is in life—in the opportunity to interact with God in everything we do. Such a life, indeed, becomes a living prayer.

When I see God in water, sun, air, everywhere, I live in reverence with everything around me because I know that if I abuse or destroy any of God's creation, I destroy my relationship with God.

ॐ

I have the possibility of a living in constant interaction with the Creator, the God of my understanding.

◄◈►◄◈►◄◈►◄◈►◄◈►◄◈►◄◈►◄◈►◄◈►◄◈►◄◈►◄◈►◄◈►◄◈►◄◈►◄◈►

REVERENCE

Our concern is about losing fishing rights. Everywhere I fish is a sanctuary to me, always been and always will be.

—*Kuhio Chandler,* Hawaiian Kupuna

Sanctuary! "Everywhere I fish is a sanctuary to me—always been and always will be."

How difficult it is for Western minds to "grok" the meaning of *sanctuary*. We have tended to believe that a sanctuary is something created by the hands of human beings. It is much more difficult for us to accept the knowing that those things given to us freely by whatever we call God are the true sanctuaries.

When we live as if this planet and everything in and on it is a natural sanctuary, including ourselves, we walk differently upon this earth.

◉

I am always on sacred ground. I must move with reverence through all Creation.

JUSTICE

Injustice needs no education. You feel it. Even the cat who is cornered will jump.

—Old Bedouin Woman

Why does justice seem so out of reach for most of the humans on this planet? Did the human experiment take a wrong turn someplace?

All of us "feel" injustice, especially when it happens to us. And if we are out of touch with our feelings, our concern about injustices to others may pass us by. Have we drugged ourselves so completely with the trappings of modern life that we can no longer *feel* injustice? Have we come to tolerate it?

All of us have been unjust at times. All of us have made mistakes. As we grow in wisdom and awareness, think what a difference it might make if each one of us made a personal commitment to seeing justice done and to taking responsibility for our own actions when we slip. It's a start.

☙❧

Justice becomes a personal issue when it is important to me.

INTERCONNECTEDNESS/ONENESS

The center of the universe is everywhere.
>—*Hehaka Sapa* (Black Elk)
>Oglala division of the Teton Dakota
>American Indian

In Western thinking, when we reflect upon the center of the universe, we do one of two things. We either try to make it "out there," in which case it becomes estranged from us, isolated from our existence, requiring us to appease and cajole it, and capable of controlling us and our destiny.

Or, in our self-centeredness, we make ourselves, our mechanistic scientific worldview, our country, and our ways the center of the universe and try to impose our ways and assumptions upon anyone or anything that differs from us.

What do we have to gain if we begin to open ourselves to the possibility that the center of the universe is everywhere?

We have the possibility of joining in with all of Creation. And by doing this we will discover that we're neither isolated from the processes of the universe nor are we responsible for everything that happens.

As we open ourselves to participating, we can begin to see the sacredness of all Creation and our place in that creation. We can begin to comprehend that our own ideas of the center of the universe are no more valid or important than those of a river or a stone.

೧೦

By respecting the "everywhereness" of the center of the universe, I come to know my own.

◄◊►◄◊►◄◊►◄◊►◄◊►◄◊►◄◊►◄◊►◄◊►◄◊►◄◊►◄◊►◄◊►◄◊►◄◊►◄◊►◄◊►

HONORING OUR BODIES/SHAME

They washed together, they got dressed in front of each other,
and there was no embarrassment.

—*Witi Ihimaera,* Maori Writer

Being comfortable with our bodies—accepting of our bodies—
being at ease with our bodies—what a gift!

This concept of ease with our bodies is often foreign to Western
people. We have learned shame and embarrassment as a form of
control. We've been taught that our bodies are evil, dirty, ugly, or
bad. Even if we think we don't believe in the "badness" of our
bodies, our behaviors and judgments belie our underlying hidden
beliefs.

Most Native people believe that our bodies were created by a
most holy God, and how could anything made by the Creator be bad?

◎

*If I am ashamed of my body, does that not mean that I am ashamed
of my Creator?*

RICHNESS

The Havai'ians spoke not only with sound but with gestures as well. A listener knew what the speaker meant by perhaps the rise of an eyebrow, an expression of the face, a tilt of the head, or a description molded with fingers. It has often been said, "Tie a kanaka's hands and you will have him tongue-tied." Many words had double, triple, and quadruple meanings, some not even remotely connected with the other. The same word pronounced one way meant one thing, yet pronounced differently it meant something else. The purport of a word depended not only upon inflection but also upon the words with which it was accompanied in a sentence.

—*Leinani Melville,* Hawaiian Kupuna

How subtle! How beautiful! How sophisticated! How complex!

How arrogant of us to think that the Hawaiians or any tribal people are primitive!

Learning the language of a people, and its true meaning is a lifetime pursuit. It asks that we be willing to let go of a system we thought contained all of reality and to expose ourselves to the infinite possibilities of learning through every pore of our being.

❧

As I constrict my life and its possibilities, I constrict a limitless soul that has infinite possibilities for being.

◄◦►◄◦►◄◦►◄◦►◄◦►◄◦►◄◦►◄◦►◄◦►◄◦►◄◦►◄◦►◄◦►◄◦►◄◦►◄◦►

LIFE AS PRAYER

I couldn't understand it then, but nothing was done unless there was a *karakia* [prayer]. It was just a whole way of life in those days, to pray.

—*Mihi Edwards,* Maori Kuia (Elder)

To live our lives as a prayer with reverence for everyone, everything, every process around us—this, I believe, is true living.

Tribal people who hold to the "old ways" are in constant prayer. Life is metered, punctuated, and embellished by prayer. Work, food gathering, healing, eating, every activity in the day is an opportunity for reverence and prayer. The gift of life itself is seen as a constant opportunity for gratitude and elicits daily prayers of thanksgiving.

When I live my life as a prayer, I am in constant touch with my Creator and my gratitude.

൭൭

When prayer is a natural part of life, life becomes a prayer. Then I know there is nothing in my life that isn't spiritual.

AMENDS

Then there's BLM [Bureau of Land Management]. They're terrible. . . . BLM comes in here to Ruby and puts on meetings. Seems like they do a lot of promising but that's about all. Like giving us a title to our land allotments. We did all our work filing for the 160 acres that each Native person over eighteen years old was entitled to. We had to have proof we lived there and used the land for so many years. Then file for it. They promised to give us title but seems like they been stalling us Natives off to legally own it. Four or five years now we been hearing them promise it'll be done next summer, next summer. We're still hearing it.

—*John Honea,* Athabaskan Elder
Ruby, Alaska

Refusing to let people have their lands when the very essence of their being is tied to the land and the land of their ancestors is like ripping out their very souls.

Only lately has the world begun to listen to the words of Native people describing how they have been dealt with by colonizing nations. As one Elder states, "It's like giving title to something handed down from the ancestors, as if the dominant society had some ownership!"

Just as Native people need their lands, we Westerners need to right our wrongs and make amends.

@@

The souls of our nations are intimately linked with the souls of individuals. Only as we begin to clean up both can we hope to live a spiritual life.

BEING HUMAN/SPIRITUALITY

A man's soul can only travel as fast as his feet can carry him.
—Old Native American Saying

Sometimes we try to get ahead of ourselves. We try to make the spiritual unworldly and ethereal. We try to remove the spiritual from the earthly and bodily aspects of ourselves. We try to find philosophies and techniques that remove us from our day-to-day existence, thinking this will make us "holy." We want to ascend. We want to transcend and transform our daily living to experience that which is beyond us.

Yet, here we are in this body, on this earthly plane, and doing what we do every day. We *are* earth. We are here—now. Our bodies, our lives, interact and are part of everything around us. It is only when we try to remove ourselves from our oneness with all things that our spirituality becomes separate and eludes us.

◉◉

My task here is to be fully human. As I embrace and live my human-ness, I know my place in the oneness.

PRESERVING THE EARTH

Earth, water, and sea belong to the gods and people are here to enhance them, not deplete them.

—Hawaiian Kupuna

I do not own the land. The land is owned by God [Akua], the Creator. Through grace, I have the privilege of being the custodian of the land for a short time as I pass through this life.

My responsibility is to enhance, enrich, and take care of the earth. The streams, lakes, and oceans are mine to look after and to make sure that they are kept clean and pure so that they can fulfill their function in the unfolding of Creation.

The air is mine to protect. Without clean air the trees will die, the gentle breezes will become killers, and the sun will fall out of relationship with the earth.

How can I fulfill my role as a person who enhances the earth, water, and sea and not be one who depletes it?

◄O►◄O►◄O►◄O►◄O►◄O►◄O►◄O►◄O►◄O►◄O►◄O►◄O►◄O►◄O►◄O►◄O►

ARROGANCE

Everyone needs to be corrected sometime, even when they're right.

—Maori Elder

In our culture, too often we overlook the role of arrogance in our everyday lives. Most of us focus on and worry about not feeling good enough, unaware that such a focus can be another form of arrogance, too.

Many years ago, I was made a pipe carrier by an old Indian chief and spiritual leader. I felt unworthy and did nothing about it for years. In part this was because I have always hated Westerners who "take on" a spiritual ritual or use a sacred teaching without having any living grounding in the culture out of which it comes. I certainly did not want to do that.

Not too long ago, I was discussing this issue with an American Indian friend, saying that I felt I should do something about being a pipe carrier. I knew I had accepted the responsibility and still I felt inadequate and unworthy.

"I can't believe you would insult that old man," my friend fired across the table at me. I burst into tears. "I would never do that!" I wailed. "Well, he chose you. Who are you to insult his choice?" she said calmly.

❧

Who are we to insult the Creator and not do the work we are here to do?

BALANCE

> Crystals are very important to the planet. There are various con-centrations of crystals around that keep the planet in balance. When these concentrations of crystals are broken up and carried off, the planet is no longer in balance.
>
> —Australian Aboriginal Elder

How little we know about the balance of the planet! Only recently in the history of Western society have we begun to be concerned about balance—balance of nature, balance of the atmosphere, balance of the oceans—balance.

The Aboriginal Elders possess a very sophisticated scientific system that we are only just beginning to probe. They have centuries of wisdom passed down through legends and stories that they are now making available to us if we will only listen.

ᕕᕗ

It is the wise person—or nation—that listens when what we need is offered to us.

SILENCE

Perhaps it [the silence of the land] is important because if we refuse to hear it, we will become other creatures.
—*Albert Wendt,* Samoan Writer

How difficult it is to listen to the silence! I remember years ago reading a book written by Lyall Watson. He was observing a Pacific-island society that experienced a lot of psychic phenomena (a Western term) in their culture. He was especially interested in an old man who was a fish finder and how he found fish. When they went out in his boat, the old fish finder slipped over the side and put his head in the water. Watson followed his example and then said, "I don't hear anything." The old fish finder said, "I know. Sometimes it's the absence of sound that's important."

ᘒ

Silence—what a rare experience! We fill up our lives with so much noise. Have we, indeed, "become other creatures"?

◄◦►◄◦►◄◦►◄◦►◄◦►◄◦►◄◦►◄◦►◄◦►◄◦►◄◦►◄◦►◄◦►◄◦►◄◦►◄◦►

SEEING TRUE

Abaganda busa bwa mbogo: bukala kungulu, sso munda mubisi.

The Baganda are like buffalo-dung: it dries on the surface, whilst it is soft underneath.

—Ugandan Proverb

Native cultures have a lot of sayings about looking honestly at treacherous friends. In fact, I always find a simple honesty in clear statements like "that person's no good" or "you can't trust that person."

In our culture, we have set up a dualism of gullibility and trusting people versus not trusting anybody. If we are nice people, we will be gullible and shut off our internal warning system, thereby trusting many people who do not deserve to be trusted. Or else we become cynical and do not trust anybody.

We have not taken responsibility for discerning the con. We do not let ourselves see below the surface. If the pile is dry on top, we step on it and then find ourselves covered with dung.

๛

Dung leaves spots. It's much easier never to get splattered with it than to try to get it off.

PREGNANCY/COMMUNITY

Well, when the woman is about four months pregnant, she starts taking these baths infused with evergreens, pure natural aromas. There are many plants the community uses for pregnant women, colds, headaches, and things like that. So the pregnant mother takes baths with plants prescribed for her by the midwife or the village leader.

—*Rigoberta Menchú*, Quiché Indian, Guatemala

Rigoberta Menchú is a Quiché Indian woman who comes from a poor village in a poor country. She has also been awarded a Nobel Peace Prize. In reading her book, *I, Rigoberta Menchú*, one is constantly confronted with the material poverty and the cultural richness of her people.

How luxuriously wealthy are the rituals that surround a pregnant Quiché woman! How beautiful are Menchú's descriptions of the awareness of the blessing of a new life about to enter this world and the ceremony and love that surround the process of pregnancy. The care of the pregnant woman and her baby in their culture does not romanticize motherhood and set up a self-centered adoration of women. Nor does it devalue the woman and her place.

The process of pregnancy firmly places the woman and the child-to-be in the community, in the traditions, and in the world, thus ensuring a sense of safety and belongingness that is grounded in the community.

When I am grounded in community, I am grounded with my God.

◄◊►◄◊►◄◊►◄◊►◄◊►◄◊►◄◊►◄◊►◄◊►◄◊►◄◊►◄◊►◄◊►◄◊►◄◊►

RELATIONSHIP TO THE LAND

Land is not just real estate, . . . land is part of the essence of who indigenous people are. It needs to be understood within the context of their spirituality and their holistic sense of creation and humanity. . . . A landless indigenous person is a person at real risk.
—*The Reverend Paul Reeves,* Maori Elder

We Westerners have a difficult time understanding what land means to indigenous people. They tell us that land is not real estate, that it is not an investment, not something to buy and sell. Land is sacred. It is the holding place for the bones of our ancestors. Land is a living and direct wellspring for our spirituality. Being bound to the land is necessary for my connection with all my ancestors and all future generations. The land places me in the context of who I am, who I have been, and who I will be. The land gives me my place. It puts me in contact with all of Creation.

ॐ

When I lose contact with my roots in the land, I am a person without a face, without a past, without a future.

THE PAST

Juze na jana si kama leo.

The day before yesterday and yesterday are not the same as today.
—Swahili Proverb

Holding on to the past and past resentments is of no use in living. It's important to learn from the past, because only then can our future be different. When we hold on to the past, we deny both our present and all the possibilities of our future.

We cannot afford to hold on to resentments. Holding on only makes us bitter and angry and robs us of the energy we need to live in the present.

@@

I change. People change. Times change. That's what living is.

TIME

God made time . . . and he made plenty of it.
—*Mrs. O'Malley,* Irish Saying

Rarely do we stop to think that "God made time." Of course, who else did? We human beings certainly did not make time. We are only born into it.

We have, however, broken it into segments, tried to make it a measurable commodity, and tried to control it.

What a wealthy idea to let ourselves luxuriate in the knowing that God has made all the time we need. There's plenty of it!

☙❧

If I have plenty of time for everything, why am I always rushing?

◄O►◄O►◄O►◄O►◄O►◄O►◄O►◄O►◄O►◄O►◄O►◄O►◄O►◄O►◄O►◄O►◄O►

CHANGING OUR LIFE ON THIS PLANET

Technologically advanced cultures dismiss the contributions of the aboriginal peoples. I believe our contribution can dramatically change everyone's life on this planet. It is imperative that people understand the separate reality of Native peoples and the rest of society.

—*Douglas Cardinal*
Canadian Indian Architect, Writer, and Artist

I know this to be true in my own life. As I have spent time with Native people throughout the world, my life and my way of living have changed dramatically.

My perspective now is much broader and less constricted. I have found a living, working, everyday spirituality that affects everything I think, do, and say. I have developed a way of being in the world that is a way of belonging with the world. And . . . I have only just begun.

☯

I am grateful that Native people are so ready to share their wisdom, and I am ready to listen.

GENOCIDE

There are few Aboriginal families in Australia, from the outback to the suburbs, who have not experienced the removal of their children. White authorities often went to great lengths to break the cultural and family bonds between parents and children. Children, even babies, were often removed to distant locations where they were arbitrarily issued with new names and birth dates. The treatment they received in institutions was often horrific.

—*Derek Fowell*, Australian Writer

What are we so afraid of? Why do we have to go to such lengths to destroy a culture—a people?

As I sit with tribal people the world over, I find that their experiences with Western culture have all been the same. Often, when I raise these issues among Westerners, I am confronted with the cry "Well, Western culture isn't the only culture that has done this!" This is the kind of reasoning I would expect to hear from a chronic alcoholic.

We *have* done this. We decry the genocide perpetrated by Hitler, yet ignore the genocide at our own doorstep.

What do we need to do to make amends? The sins of the fathers are, indeed, visited upon the sons and the daughters.

@&

Awareness without action lacks sincerity. Are we as a culture open to what we have to learn? Truly, we need to be more afraid of ourselves than of Native cultures.

HEALING

Oliver Amouak and his wife used to use stinkweed. Their daughter still collects it for them. It grows all around here. They take a bath with it and drink it in tea and juice. Olga and Oliver Amouak are old but they're hardly ever sick. They say it's a cure-all for almost everything, even for cancer. . . . Just think, so many things right here and we don't practice using it.

—*Josephine Roberts,* Athabaskan Elder
Tanana, Alaska

We have finally started to notice that there is real curative value in local herbs and remedies. In fact, we are also becoming aware that there are little or no side effects to most natural remedies, and that they are often more effective than Western medicine.

In listening to old people, I hear many tales of the church and the Western authorities telling them that their healings are evil and sorcery and that they are forbidden to practice healing in the old way. What kinds of minds have tried to eliminate effective forms of healing in favor of a "one party" system?

ॐ

The Old Ones probably have many ways to help us be healthier than we are. We have only to listen.

VARIETY AND RICHNESS

We need the knowledge the *Paheka* [white people] brings from all over the world as well as the sense of belonging and the *whakapapa* [genealogy/history/culture] of the Maori. The separate paths our people have trod can unite in a highway to the future that is built on the best of both. Maori and *Paheka*, alone and divided, cannot build a secure and happy future for Aotearoa [New Zealand].

—*Dame Whina Cooper*
Maori Kuia (Elder) and Stateswoman

What is it about Western culture that sets up the desire to destroy everything that is unlike itself or to turn every other culture and its people into a reproduction of itself? I believe this process has evolved because Western culture is based on a belief system that is closed, and closed systems, by their very nature, cannot tolerate the existence of other cultures.

The Maori have taken a strong stand that in order for Aotearoa (New Zealand) to realize its full potential, it must, as a country, honor, value, and preserve its bicultural heritage.

The world becomes richer as we recognize that each of our cultures is only a piece of a rich crazy quilt. How dull our planet would become if, over time, all the pieces became one color and one pattern.

☺

Tribal cultures, like endangered species and plants, may be the key to our survival as a planet.

◄O►◄O►◄O►◄O►◄O►◄O►◄O►◄O►◄O►◄O►◄O►◄O►◄O►◄O►◄O►◄O►◄O►◄O►

DEATH/HEALTH

When they were ready to leave, they called the family together and they checked out. There was rejoicing. There was no illness, no sadness. When my grandmother was ready to leave, there was no illness. She called us all together. They were in touch with the *aumakua* [spiritual ancestors].

—*Angeline Locey,* Hawaiian Kupuna

Again and again Native people tell us, "We were healthy until the White people came. Our people lived to be a hundred and fifty or more, in health, before contact [before the invasion]." Rarely do we Westerners stop to ask, "How many of the diseases we suffer from are culturally based?" We have bought into the belief that Western medicine is eradicating illness, but just how many illnesses are *caused* by Western medicine and the Western mechanistic science? Native people the world over believe there are quite a few.

How much of our cancer epidemic is being caused by toxins in our air, water, food, and artificial chemicals? Native people believe it is a lot.

How much of our psychological and spiritual illnesses are caused by our estrangement from ourselves, from one another, from nature, from our dead ancestors, and from the God of our knowing? Native people are asking these questions.

◎◉

As I open myself to questions being posed by those from other systems, I gain perspective on how many of my beliefs are system based.

CIVILIZATION

The man who sat on the ground in his tipi meditating on life and its meaning, accepting the kinship of all creatures and acknowledging unity with the universe of things, was infusing into his being the true essence of civilization.

—*Chief Luther Standing Bear*
Oglala (Teton) Sioux
American Indian

How many of us believe that to be civilized means to possess "things" and technology, to espouse Western theology and belief systems, and to be educated in abstract thinking?

Doesn't "civilization" mean, as Chief Luther Standing Bear has said, to accept our place in "the kinship of all creatures" and the "unity with the universe"?

When we realize that we are, indeed, one with others, we become less willing to destroy them, because we understand that we are, in essence, destroying ourselves.

Doesn't true "civilization" mean rising above petty differences and divisions and seeing the whole picture? Doesn't it mean having the humility to know that we are only *part* of it?

☺

If I revise my idea of what is "civilized," I might come closer to my Creator.

WARRIORS

It is this warrior mentality that most characterizes the Celt, though it is warrior in a very specific sense. The warrior was the one who brought in the new age, the transition person. The agent of change.

—*Daniel Martin,* Irish/Celtic Writer

It is much more difficult to try to change a system with words than it is by the sword. Yet, where would we be without those who have had the courage to "blow the whistle"? Where would we be if we did not have those brave souls who stand up to say, "There's something wrong here and we have to change"?

If there is any group of people that have consistently demonstrated courage, through the centuries, it is the Irish. What can we learn from a people for whom the warrior was the "one who brought in the new age"?

We are living in a time of the beginnings of massive change. Who are our warriors?

THE EARTH

We must respect our Mother, the Earth, or we can never grow as human beings, her children.

—*Phil Lane, Sr.,* Yankton Lakota Elder
American Indian

Mother Earth. The earth provides. It is so easy to interpret offering gratitude to the earth as a pagan form of idol worship. I know I used to think it was a bit silly to worship the earth. How else was a Western mind to think? Also, was that not an affront to the one true God?

However, as I began to sit with Native people and to share their lives, I developed a totally different perspective. For example, I experience very little "worship" in tribal people, as Westerners describe and experience worship. Worship in a Western sense, I have come to see, means a one-up/one-down relationship of subservience.

What we Westerners interpret as worship is simply not possible when we are participating with the Creator in the universe. I have experienced most tribal people as just being grateful for reality.

Where does my food come from? Directly or indirectly, it comes from the earth. I need to recognize that fact and be grateful.

What makes the plants grow, therefore feeding all on the earth? The sun is necessary for that process. And where would all this growing be without water? Nowhere. I need to acknowledge my gratitude for the sun and water and not take water for granted.

❦

In earth, air, sun, and water, I see the fine hand of the Creator. Without these treasures, I would not be here to give thanks.

SPIRITUAL LIVING

To me as a tribal Aboriginal, dreaming is more than just an ordinary dream which one would dream at night or day. To us, dreaming is reality, because it takes in all the Aboriginal spirituality. When the religious tribal elders say, "This mountain is my dreaming," or "that land is my dreaming," he is really saying to us that this mountain or that land holds very sacred knowledge, wisdom and moral teaching, passed on to us by the spirit of the Creator, who has created for us the holy sacred sites and the sacred mountains which exist today.

—Australian Aboriginal

I find it difficult to understand with my brain what the Australian Aboriginal means by his "dreaming." Regardless of how much I listen to Aboriginals talk about their dreaming or read about Dreamtime, I'm not sure I will ever really understand, at least with my mind. I have read many accounts by anthropologists and Western writers that are almost laughable.

Yet, one time when I was sitting with a group of Aboriginal Elders who were talking about their ways and beliefs, my inner being suddenly understood. I sat there with tears streaming down my face, knowing that when they talked about dreaming they were talking about what I am trying to articulate when I talk about Living in Process.

I have often said that Living in Process is something we already know. We have been trained to unlearn it.

@@

Our inner beings know how to live fully and how to live as one with all things. It is a gift from our Creator.

OPENNESS

We are all brothers and sisters in the Hawaiian culture. It is not the color of the skin or blood that determines Hawaiians . . . it is the color of the heart.

—*Alex Pua*, Hawaiian Kupuna

I am Hawaiian. My Hawaiian friends tell me I am Hawaiian because I have a Hawaiian heart.

People who are intimately tuned in to the oneness of all things have little difficulty letting others seemingly unlike themselves into their hearts.

A Hawaiian heart is open, honest, humble, courageous, clear, nonjudgmental, accepting, and in touch with the Creator.

Have you ever noticed how people of color and tribal people have an immediate connection when they meet that transcends racial groups, color, or nationality?

☙❧

I welcome the richness and life-enhancing lessons I learn from tribal peoples.

◄◊►◄◊►◄◊►◄◊►◄◊►◄◊►◄◊►◄◊►◄◊►◄◊►◄◊►◄◊►◄◊►◄◊►◄◊►◄◊►

WEALTH/POVERTY/CULTURE

In some way, I think we were rich anyway. We had the sand-
dunes to play in and our lovely big harbour. We had our culture.
—*Mira Szaszy*, Maori Kuia (Elder)

We have some very strange ideas about wealth and poverty in
Western culture. Somehow we have come to believe that wealth
has something to do with money and possessions. This is a particularly Western concept. How arrogant of us to call people poor simply because they have little money!

Ironically there seems to be some correlation between having
lots of money and being "poor in spirit"—at least many spiritual
teachers warn us of that possibility.

What if being poor is not knowing and not having one's own
culture? What if being poor is not being rooted in the culture and
earth of one's ancestors?

◉◊

*I am wealthy when I touch the earth around me, when I know my
roots, and when I am grounded in a culture that nourishes me.*

MARCH

CHILD REARING

All brothers of the same parents should regard all their children as one, and consequently should treat them alike after the fashion of one's own children.

—*Asesela Ravuvu*, Fijian Writer

How rich I would have been if all my father's brothers had regarded me as their daughter! There were four brothers, all with different personalities, different skills, different outlooks on life, and all married to different women.

I was an only child. Brothers and sisters would have been such a luxury. And my belonging would have been so much more secure.

☯

Wealth may be simply having several mothers and fathers.

OPEN HEARTS

I believe much trouble and blood would be saved if we opened our hearts more.

—*Hin-mah-too-yah-lat-kekht (Chief Joseph)*
Nez Percé
American Indian

So do I.

Chief Joseph was such an amazing man. I grew up in "his" country and his words surrounded me as a child.

Opening our hearts in a crazy society can be dangerous, yet can we afford not to?

Indian people have been slaughtered physically, emotionally, financially, and personally by opening their hearts, and yet they continue to do it. Even though opening our hearts is dangerous, how much more dangerous is it to threaten our souls by refusing?

I feel so good about myself when I open my heart.

EATING/HUMOR

We Hawaiians don't eat until we are full, we eat until we are tired. . . . So eat up, and take a rest if you need to.
—Hawaiian Woman

I have never known Native people who did not laugh and joke about themselves! Humor in Native cultures is as natural as breathing. Teasing, joking, laughing, and poking fun are a normal part of daily life.

Also, this kind of humor is always harmless. It is never full of barbs, put-downs, or judgments. It is often simple, fun, and easy.

Humor among tribal people is intimacy. In the joking and laughing, we touch, rub, caress, and get to know one another.

◎◎

I like to laugh. I like to play. I like to roll around, verbally, with my human family.

◄O►◄O►◄O►◄O►◄O►◄O►◄O►◄O►◄O►◄O►◄O►◄O►◄O►◄O►◄O►◄O►◄O►

VOLUNTEERING/WORKING

We work volunteer—you could never get people to work this hard if you paid them for it.

—*Bruce Stewart,* Maori Elder

That's true! We are much more willing to work from our hearts than for money. Isn't it strange that our materialistic world has not discovered this sooner?

When we volunteer for something, we've already made a commitment to it. The work that follows is just a logical conclusion of a previously made decision.

When we do the work of the Creator, and when our work flows out of a previously made decision to work for our Creator, the money follows. We have only to take the next steps required of us, and life follows.

◉◉

I entered life as a volunteer. My work is just a follow-up.

◄O► ◄O► ◄O► ◄O► ◄O► ◄O► ◄O► ◄O► ◄O► ◄O► ◄O► ◄O► ◄O► ◄O► ◄O► ◄O► ◄O►

FEELINGS

When the pipes and tobacco were placed on the kitchen table, Mary Doogan burst into a passionate fit of weeping. The neighbour women were glad she cried. "Let her empty her heart," Mary Manus said, with a knowledge of the day she had cried for her drowned son, in her mind to give her wisdom.
—*Peadar O'Donnell,* Irish Writer

What a relief to be with people who know how important feelings are and how important it is to let them flow out of us!

The Irish have always been noted for being a feeling lot. Life is experienced passionately and intensely.

Feelings are one of the gifts of being human. They are there for our awareness and our healing. It would be a shame to miss them now, wouldn't it?

❧

Feelings are never inappropriate—just sometimes inappropriately placed.

OUR ELDERS/OUR TREASURE

Old people are highly respected, honoured and loved. They are regarded as the living links with the ancestors.
—*Feleti E. Ngan-Woo,* Samoan Writer

The Elders are our link with our ancestors. We need to have a living knowledge of that link to understand our culture, to feel our roots, and to live our lives. Our Elders give us our grounding. They give us a perspective that comes only with age and wisdom. Not only that, our Elders have intimate knowledge of a time before the one in which we are living, and they still carry information from their Elders about a world we can never really know, although our times are still influenced by those who have gone before.

Also, in the very process of loving, honoring, and respecting our Elders, we are changed.

෨෨

My Elders are great teachers. When I use them as a sounding board, I gain a necessary perspective.

WOMEN'S ROLES

The assumptions that were made about the roles of Aboriginal women by these men were based on gross misconceptions. Women were regarded as having little authority in Aboriginal society. Such observations were made by the white men imposing their own cultural values on Aboriginal society.

—*Maggie Kavanagh*

When tribal people observe Western culture, they often state that the women and their work seem to have no value and that this bias is projected onto them as well.

In Western culture, women seem to believe that to be of value, they need to be of value in the same way men are.

What have we to learn from a culture where all work is valued and people are valued as they do it?

@D

We have a lot to learn about what would happen if women were women and men were men and each did the work they were called to do.

FEAR

The God of evil and the God of fear are good friends.

—Maori Proverb

I have struggled with this proverb. The minute I saw it, I knew it was important, and I have difficulty putting into words the "knowing" that I felt in my being.

I do know that when I am living out of fear, I am vulnerable to evil. I know that fear builds on itself and turns on itself. I know that when I am afraid, I am out of touch with the healing of my God and am more vulnerable to being manipulated and controlled.

I know that when I am in fear, I forget that I am loved and protected and that my life is as it should be.

Fear is my signal that I have abandoned all the gods that protect and guide me.

<o><o><o><o><o><o><o><o><o><o><o><o><o><o><o>

BROADENING OUR PERSPECTIVE

Primal cultures are essentially much alike, as proved by the universality of their myths; but worldviews, beliefs, and attitudes of primal societies are so fundamentally different from those of the modern Western society that what may be perfectly logical to one group may seem bizarre and incomprehensible to the other.
—*Herb Kawainui Kane*
Hawaiian Kupuna and Artist

Actually, this is what this book is all about. My hope is that if we Westerners sit down with Native wisdom from all over the world day after day, we may begin to understand that our worldview needs the knowledge that tribal people have to share with us at this point in the evolution of the planet.

We have developed a system that sees differences as a threat. Yet, I have learned from my own journey that it is possible for Western minds, over time, to shift our perception to a more life-giving way of being in the world.

༺༻

We have a window—a door! Before these people are destroyed completely, it's up to us to open our hearts and minds to new knowledge.

◄◊►◄◊►◄◊►◄◊►◄◊►◄◊►◄◊►◄◊►◄◊►◄◊►◄◊►◄◊►◄◊►◄◊►◄◊►◄◊►

A QUESTION OF LOVE

We have called you onto our *marae* [sacred place/meeting house/gathering place]. From now on you are *whanau* [family]. You are always welcome here.

—Maori Elder

Whanau has become almost a sacred word to me. How many times in how many places among the Maori people of New Zealand have I heard and experienced that I am *whanau*, that I am family?

Every *marae* that has called me on has welcomed me as *whanau* and I am free to return, to stay, to sleep, to eat, and I am welcomed as long, lost family. This is the way I grew up in a small town in "Indian Territory" in Oklahoma. My family always welcomed everyone who wanted to be as family. It's a good way to live.

I have discovered that this attitude is suspect in white Western culture. In fact, I had the following conversation with a reporter recently:

"I notice that you really seem to love the people in your Living Process Network."

"Yes, I do."

"And I notice that they really seem to love you."

"Yes, they do."

"Don't you think there's something wrong with that?"

What's wrong with this picture?

@

We are all whanau [*family*] *to the Creator.*

INTERGENERATIONAL KNOWING

> You missed your grandmothers. I was very, very close to my
> grandmothers and I missed them terribly.
> —*Iris Clayton*, Australian Aboriginal

This statement was made by a woman who was taken from her family and placed in a mission compound, a home for Aboriginal girls, the Cootamundra Girls' Home in New South Wales.

When I read this statement, I remembered how very, very important my great-grandmother was in my life. My earliest childhood memory is of her tenderness with me.

I am aware how important it is to have older people in our lives. Our grandmothers and grandfathers have so much wisdom that spans so much living. We lose perspective with one- or two-generational living.

@@

Elders add richness and texture to our lives. There are always Elders to be found, regardless of where we may be.

◀o▶◀o▶◀o▶◀o▶◀o▶◀o▶◀o▶◀o▶◀o▶◀o▶◀o▶◀o▶◀o▶◀o▶◀o▶◀o▶

COMMUNITY

"We" overrides "me."

—Hawaiian Proverb

Tribal peoples know how to be a community. In Western culture, we have tried to make the nuclear family the building block of culture and have seen again and again that this small unit cannot possibly meet the needs of its individual members.

Recently, I heard a lawyer and a tax consultant discussing the fact that the tax laws, and other laws of our land, actually militate against trust and community. Much of what we have set up in our system serves to isolate and alienate.

We are afraid of intimacy. We are afraid of having and needing one another. We are afraid of getting too close. We are afraid of asking for help. Often, we don't even know that community is what we need.

૭૭

We are community. We are one. Why do we fight it so?

RESOURCES/WASTEFULNESS

Mufumbya-gganda: tabalirira mutyabi.

One who uses a big bundle of firewood for cooking has no consideration for one who has to gather the firewood.

—Ugandan Proverb

Somehow, the use of limited resources might be better understood if there were a closer relationship between those who gather the resources and those who use them. One who does not work himself does not understand how hard it is.

The United States uses a very large percentage of the resources of the entire world. Yet, most of our lives are very far removed from the production and gathering of those resources. Tribal people have stayed much closer to the link between production and usage. Perhaps not all of us can arrange our lives to be as close to the production of what we need as tribal peoples are. Still, we can listen to what those who are closer to the earth and her bounty know and are saying. And we can translate this knowledge in our everyday living.

๏๏

One of the ways that I block the learnings available to me is to think that I can learn only from those who are "like me."

HUMILITY

I'm no expert working on birch or anything like that, but I know how to pick out good birch to make sleds and things.
—*John Honea,* Athabaskan Elder
Ruby, Alaska

We have a lot to learn about humility from Native people. Native humility is almost always a quiet acceptance of who the person is. No pomp and circumstance, just facts.

There is something lovely about this quiet humility. There is a simple acceptance of life on life's terms. I have never heard bragging or false humility. Most often what I hear is the truth.

How refreshing! A truthful awareness of who one is, which means quietly owning when one is not skilled and just as quietly owning when one is very skilled. I have been battered for this truth in Western culture, yet tribal people seem comfortable with the truth.

☯

When I express the simple truth of who I am, I feel clear and whole.

OLD WAYS/LEARNING

We go by the old time marks when we fish. I never used a depth recorder because I always found plenty fish by the old time marks.

—*Kaipo Chandler*, Hawaiian Kupuna

Kaipo Chandler is a friend, a famous Hawaiian fisherman, and a Kupuna. I feel privileged to know him and to call him "friend."

I have spent many hours listening to him talk about the old ways and the old knowings. What he knows about fishing cannot be learned in a book, nor can it be taught in classes. His is a knowing that comes from living with, participating with, and noticing with teachers who have taken hours, days, months, and years to teach what they know. His is the kind of wisdom that can't be taught in a hurry.

❦

A meaningful life is surely one that allows for learnings that evolve slowly.

LIVING FULLY

In Samoa it is difficult to accept death—everything invites you to live.

—*Albert Wendt,* Samoan Writer

How important our environment is to us! Beauty, nature, the oceans, the trees, the fragrance of the flowers all invite us to live life to its fullest.

How important it is to make the environment in which we live life supporting. This feeling of the fullness of life is difficult to generate when one is surrounded by steel and concrete.

❧

Nature is such a great teacher for living. I need to spend time with my teacher.

WISDOM

The wisest man sees the least, says the least, but prays the most.
—Irish Proverb

Sure, and 'tis the Irish who learn that wisdom is knowing when to keep our mouths shut.

How is it that we have come to equate wisdom with managing the system and with academic achievement? This is not wisdom. This is manipulation of people and information.

Wisdom is a personal process, usually between us and our God.

When I keep my mouth shut and listen, I learn so much more. Being with Elders has taught me that if I need to convince people how much I know, I'm in trouble. I can offer everything I have to give and wait to give it until it is asked for.

※

Wisdom is about living. It is not about things.

◄O►◄O►◄O►◄O►◄O►◄O►◄O►◄O►◄O►◄O►◄O►◄O►◄O►◄O►◄O►◄O►◄O►

INTIMACY

Unfortunately, white people can never understand the beauty, the closeness of being black. When you are black, you are never alone.

—Australian Aboriginal
One of seven contributors to
The Spirit of Musgrave Park

One of the things I noticed when I was a child growing up in the South was that whenever black people came together, even if they were strangers, they always seemed to "know" one another. They were like "family." There was a closeness, a belonging, a knowing.

I have always envied this intimacy and wished for it for myself. As I travel, I see this same phenomenon in tribal people the world over. Amazingly enough, I have seen indigenous people express the same connectedness toward people from very different cultures as much as to one another. This intimacy seems to be related more to a philosophy of life than to being part of a particular group.

@@

How lonely I feel in a culture that is built on escape from intimacy. I have much to learn.

◁◦▷◁◦▷◁◦▷◁◦▷◁◦▷◁◦▷◁◦▷◁◦▷◁◦▷◁◦▷◁◦▷◁◦▷◁◦▷◁◦▷◁◦▷◁◦▷

PRESERVING INDIGENOUS CULTURES

We share the war to preserve our indigenous cultures.
—Woman from Peru

Throughout the world, there is a struggle to preserve indigenous cultures. Usually, these battles are fought by small groups of indigenous people who have organized and banded together not only to save their lives but to save their way of life for future generations.

We, as people of this planet, have difficulty realizing that their struggle is our struggle. We need their perspective to broaden our own. We need their knowledge of healing to help us see alternatives to our Western medical view, which is not only very limited but may also be causing as many problems as it is healing. We need the political, familial, and community perspective of indigenous people to help us heal some of our social ills.

☙

How much easier it would be for indigenous people to save their cultures if we Westerners realized that we need them in order for us all to survive and thrive on this planet!

ORAL POETRY

[We want to save] ". . . that which is written on the people's tongues."

—*Peter Kalifornsky,* Dena'ina Elder
Alaska

What a beautiful phrase: "that which is written on the people's tongues."

The poetry of the spoken language is like the smell of sweetgrass in the sweat lodge, the touch of mist on our eyelids, and the longing for healing in our hearts.

How important it is to preserve a cultural heritage that is oral and the very knowledge of the power of language itself, so that we can reunite the puzzle pieces of our shattered planet when the time is right.

❧

I am grateful for the poetry that is written on the people's tongues.

WORDS/APPRECIATION OF ANOTHER

Words have great power and should be used carefully. *Aloha,* for example, should not be seen as just a frivolous tourist greeting. *Alo* means the bosom of center of the universe, and *ha,* the breath of God, so to say this word is to appreciate another person's divinity.

—*Nana Veary,* Hawaiian Kupuna

"To appreciate another person's divinity" . . . it hardly seems that anything more needs to be said. What an act of grace to recognize and appreciate another's divinity. How our world would change with that one small act.

Rarely do we stop to realize the possible implications and/or repercussions of the words that issue from our mouths. We need to be responsible for what goes in our mouths, and we need to be responsible for what comes out of our mouths. The second is much harder.

☙

May the words of my mouth and the meditations of my heart appreciate the divinity in everyone.

ATTRIBUTES OF A CELTIC WARRIOR

The associated attributes [of the Celtic warrior mentality] illustrate this particular understanding [that warriors were agents of change]: respect, awareness of fear, wakefulness, and self-confidence.
                                        —*Daniel Martin,* Irish Writer

Of all the Western cultures, the Irish are the closest to tribal people. How similar the Celtic warrior is to persons who are held in high esteem in other tribal groups.

The warrior should have respect for all. Respect is not a common commodity in our modern world. Fear, yes. Awe, yes. One-downmanship, yes. Respect, rarely. And respectfulness is such an important way of being in this world.

Awareness of fear: We must be in touch with our feelings and recognize that our feelings are often the only warning we have of imminent danger. We need to be aware when we feel afraid and to honor our fear. Only then can we be truly courageous.

Wakefulness: A warrior needs to be present, neither living for the past nor yearning for the future. Only a person living in the present can know what is needed for change.

Self-confidence: When we are sure we are here to do the Creator's work and have put ego aside, there is no reason not to have self-confidence.

☯

Respect, awareness of fear, wakefulness, and self-confidence: I can wear these attributes well.

BALANCE/LEARNING

A good heart and a good mind—these are what you need to be a chief.

—*Louis Farmer,* Onondaga Elder
American Indian

The mind is a gift. It helps us to process and understand ourselves and the world around us. Our minds can learn in many ways. We can learn abstractly, we can learn from experience, we can learn by listening to and watching others, we can learn from mistakes, and we can learn from successes.

Yet, without the balance of the heart, the mind is an enslaving master. Only through the heart can the mind be balanced. Our hearts teach us of the unknown, of that which is glimpsed only darkly, and of what is real and important.

Why would I have been given a whole being if I am not expected to use it?

☯

A mind that is not balanced by the heart is a tyrant. A heart that is not balanced by the mind is ineffectual.

RECONNECTING

We cannot depend on governments to heal our wounds. We have to help each other.

—*Hene,* Maori Woman Elder

People at the grassroots level are the only ones who can change the direction Western culture has taken.

It is only as we reach out to one another across barriers of race, nationality, political systems, and beliefs that we can connect the severed and heal the broken.

We people of the world are one people. We belong to a creation and a universe that lives and breathes as one organism.

Only we can rejoin ourselves.

KEEPER OF MY SOUL

Other people can rape and damage my body. Only I can damage my soul.

—American Indian Woman Elder

Only I can damage my soul. I have heard Native people talk about rape, beatings, and torture in boarding schools. These they withstood, usually with quiet resolve. This time in their history was horrible. Few Native families have not been touched by these boarding-school experiences.

Yet, most Native people I know have come to believe that these experiences made them stronger. They survived, and their culture survived. Now they can come forward and speak in these times about which their legends have spoken.

If we ourselves do not damage our souls, no one else can. Our envelopes, our bodies, can be tortured, yet we ourselves are responsible for any damage our souls suffer.

I am the keeper of my soul. The Creator and I work hand in hand in this task.

WORK

Work is regarded as an ennobling virtue. Through work a person gains the respect and admiration of family and the larger community.

—*Cleve Barlow*, Maori Writer

We hear very little of vocation in Western culture today. Work is often narrowly seen as the way we support our materialism. The ideas in a book such as *Do What You Love, The Money Will Follow* seem extraordinary and unique.

There is a belief that only the privileged have the luxury of seeing work as an "ennobling virtue."

If I cannot see my work as "ennobling," I cannot respect myself. And if I do not respect myself, how can anything I do be noble?

※

When I have my place in the family and community, I have support for my contribution.

MISTAKES

The Creator designed us to learn by trial and error. The path of life we walk is very wide. Everything on the path is sacred—what we do right is sacred—but our mistakes are also sacred. This is the Creator's way of teaching spiritual people. To criticize ourselves when we make mistakes is not the Indian way. To learn from our mistakes is the Indian way. The definition of a spiritual person is someone who makes 30–50 mistakes each day and talks to the Creator after each one to see what to do next time. This is the way of the warrior.

—*Don Coyhis*, Mohican Writer and Consultant
American Indian

There is no way to walk our path and not make mistakes. We Westerners are often told that we *are* our mistakes or even that we *are* a mistake. This is not the Indian way.

We only have mistakes in our life so that we can learn. The bigger our mistakes, the greater our possibilities for learning.

However, we are not alone in our mistakes. When we seek counsel with the Great Spirit after each one, we don't need to do that one again.

❀

When I accept that I make mistakes and I am not a *mistake, I am on the spiritual path.*

◄◊►◄◊►◄◊►◄◊►◄◊►◄◊►◄◊►◄◊►◄◊►◄◊►◄◊►◄◊►◄◊►◄◊►◄◊►◄◊►◄◊►

LIVING ART

A lot of tribes don't have a word for "art" in their language because it is so much a part of their culture.
                                    —Young Native American Elder

Think of it! There are so many words that do not appear in Native
cultures—not because these cultures are primitive or unsophisti-
cated, as was thought in the past, but because the actions that we
use words to describe are so integrated into the everyday life of the
people that they are not conceived of separately.

When our lives are surrounded by beauty and creativity, we
walk differently upon this earth.

The greatest art of all is that of the Creator. As I gaze out my
window across the meadows and stream toward the mountains, I
am surrounded by an artistic creation that stirs my soul.

๑๏

*The mountains circle their arms around me here. The meadow pro-
vides a calm place through which a stream composes music. The Creator blesses me today with a world that nourishes me. Thank you.*

GIFTS/HUMILITY

I want to thank the Creator for all His gifts. I don't always understand the gifts of those who say negative things about me and
who attack me, and I do trust that the Creator has given me these
gifts so that I can learn and grow spiritually.

—*Lenore Stiffarm,* Poet and Professor
Blood Tribe
Canada

I find it difficult to pray for those who attack me and to accept
their attacks as gifts. Yet, I have heard again and again from my
American Indian sisters and brothers that we can only thank the
Creator for whatever is bestowed upon us. My Native mentors do
not ask me not to feel the pain or anger that comes with attacks.
They only offer the possibility that everything that comes to us
comes from the Creator and is therefore a gift.

❧

*When I accept the whole range of gifts from my Creator, I am ready
for the school of life.*

MITAKUYE OYASIN—FOR ALL OUR RELATIONS

Whenever we pray we always pray *"mitakuye oyasin,"* for all our relations. We pray for all of the black people, all the yellow people, all the white people, and all the red people. We pray for all our relations.

—Lakota Elder
American Indian

I heard this statement many times growing up, and I am aware of the four directions and the four colors (red, yellow, black, and white). I have heard prayers ended with *mitakuye oyasin* and have joined in with "for all our relations." Yet, somehow, from my Western perspective, I always assumed that "for all my relations" meant my *family*—extended at best.

Then, as I visited tribal people globally and felt their struggle for the survival of their people and their culture, and reflected on my experience of Christian prayers, I realized that the American Indians are the only people I know who regularly pray for all people of the earth . . . people of every color.

Then I realized that I have this whole group of people—most of whom are unknown to me—praying for me all the time. They have done it for years. It is not a simple "praying for my enemies." It is a praying for my family . . . those with whom I am intimate . . . those with whom I am connected, those whom I love, whether I know them personally or not. All my relations.

Perhaps the prayers that most influence us are those that are unknown to us.

DIFFERENCES

Kiwekwacho na Mungu, mwanadamu hawezi kukiondoa.

What God has established, man cannot annul.

— Swahili Proverb

What God has established, man cannot annul! I wonder how often do we stop and ponder what God has established . . . the earth, the trees, the plants, clean air, clean water?

I wonder, do we ever really stop to think that we have different cultures, different languages, different perspectives on this planet for a reason? Have we ever stopped to imagine that differences are a gift?

Why would we try to annul the rich heritage of variability we have on this planet to develop a one-party system?

❧

When a rainbow gets constricted, it becomes one color—white.

APRIL

INCLUSION

If you are a part of my nephew's whanau, you are a part of my whanau so let's all stay and talk together.
—*Uncle Henry,* Maori Elder
Banks Peninsula

In Maori, *whanau* means family and even more than family. It means being taken in as brother or sister or auntie. It means being included.

I have been so grateful to be included in many Maori families and treated as if I were Maori. "If your heart is Maori, then you are Maori. You are one of us."

I am aware that so much of Western culture is built upon exclusion. "This is *my* family. I only trust *my* family."

I wasn't raised that way, and I'm beginning to see that I was not raised for this culture. My Irish mother was always ready to share what we had with others—and it often wasn't much—and to include them in our family. I have discovered that inclusion is looked upon with suspicion in Western culture, frowned upon, and often seen as "bad."

☮

How nice it is to be included—and to include others.

CHOOSING LIFE

I started drinking more seriously, seeking refuge, seeking death actually, from a world that was feeling more and more unnatural to me. Following a painful accident related to drinking, I finally realized that I must decide whether I want to follow my grandparents or to truly take up this life. Circumstances that followed led me to choose life.

—*Barney Bush,* Shawnee Elder
American Indian

Alcohol and drug abuse is a terrible problem for Native people throughout the world. Every colonizing nation has introduced alcohol and drugs to the Native people, which have destroyed their families, their cultures, and their spirituality.

For many Native people, as for many Westerners, alcohol and drugs have been welcome sedatives that shut off the pain of living in an "unnatural" and destructive system. The issue with addiction is "Do I want to numb myself and fit into the system?" If that is not a viable alternative, the issue becomes "Do I want to take up this life?"

@O

When I choose life, I choose myself. I choose Creation.

WE COME FROM GOD

We emanated from divine origin in the Kingdom of God. This privileged arrangement did not go over too well with those who believed man was molded from dust of this earth and who figured that they had the only option on the heavenly market.

—*Leinani Melville*, Hawaiian Kupuna

How sensible to believe that we come from God and that we return to God. It is so much easier to participate in our oneness when we know that we all emanate from the same source—that we, too, are divine. This way we don't get confused and exhausted by spiritual competition. We all belong.

When I see the divinity in another, I am more likely to experience my own.

RESPONSIBILITY

Even though a person may work for a living, they must also devote time and effort to the care of their home and family. This is the true measure of an industrious person.

— *Cleve Barlow,* Maori Writer

In Maori culture, the home and the family are very important. "Getting ahead" is not just making a lot of money or being successful. Success and right living are dependent upon devotion to family and home. If you have a lot of money and have not taken care of your home and your extended family, you are not seen to be a "good" person.

🌀

Being an industrious person means moving beyond our self-centered need to produce.

◄◎►◄◎►◄◎►◄◎►◄◎►◄◎►◄◎►◄◎►◄◎►◄◎►◄◎►◄◎►◄◎►◄◎►◄◎►◄◎►

COMMUNICATION

My wife and I worked together mostly. That's how we happened to do so well. We both worked together every way and agreed with everything we've done, so that way along on life, it was very easy for us.

—*John Honea,* Athabaskan Elder
Ruby, Alaska

Just reading John Honea's words, I felt a peace—a peace about his relationship with his wife and their relationship with each other. How easy life would be if we all worked together that way. How easy life would be if we learned to agree and to be with one another, not to exploit one another.

I have learned that when I take the responsibility to get clear about what I want and then state it concisely—not as a demand, rather as a statement—and the other person does the same, and both of us take responsibility for our decisions, things go very well.

The breakdown comes when one or the other of us doesn't get clear, doesn't state what we want in a negotiable and clear way, or doesn't take responsibility for the consequences of our decision.

◎◑

My life is much simpler when I get clear about what I want.

GOD PROVIDES

One day I was seeing a patient in my little clinic and needed an herb. The herbs I used were 90 percent indigenous to Guatemala, as were the people I treated. I remember researching my herb books and the specific herb I needed I had learned in school at the Institute in Santa Lucia Milpas Altas, but I had not seen it since. Señor Castro was outside weaving sticks together with a vine to make a fence. I left my patient and went out to ask him if he knew where I could find that herb. *"Pues, pero aquí esta!"* ("Well, here it is!") *"Dios se lo da lo que necesitas!"* ("God gives you what you need!") And, sure enough, the vine Señor Castro was using was the herb I needed!

—*Señor Castro,* Guatemalan Indian Elder
        As recounted by Latifa Amdur, L.Ac, Dipl. Ac., and C.H.

Living a life of faith is very difficult for those of us who down deep believe that we are the ones in control. Yet, living a life of faith is what is required to walk the path of a spiritual life. When we get down on our knees and ask God for the next right step, the answer is not multiple choice. The first answer we get is what we need, and we have to trust that.

☙❧

Living a life of faith is what living is.

PARTICIPATION/BUILDING AND DEPLETING

Alciwa mkazi jinga.

If you come to stay—build!

—Swahili Proverb

When we come to build, we do not have to deplete or destroy. Many of us have become unconscious of how much of what we do is motivated by the urge to destroy, to use, and to use up.

When we live gently with the earth and the people around us, we realize that our lives have meaning only when they emanate from a spiritual base and we are committed to building and healing.

What a different world we would live in if all corporate decisions started with what would be healing for the planet and for individuals! What an amazing world it would be if, when we receive a hurt from another, we did not lash out but responded only when we were clear about what would be healing to the other and to ourselves.

Somehow, we have convinced ourselves that we have to destroy in order to heal.

❧

What if we found a way of building to heal?

TRUST

Our white relatives say the Indian is stoic. This is not necessarily
true. We just wait to see the true person. Given time, he will
show his true self, so we wait and time will provide the proof.
      —*Phil Lane, Sr.,* Yankton Lakota Elder
      American Indian

Perhaps this is why I feel so honored to be family with Phil Lane,
Sr. I know that he waited to see if his heart knew he could trust me,
and then he made his decision. I do not have to worry that Phil is a
"fair-weather friend" or someone who will go away. There is no
"instant intimacy" among traditional American Indians. There is
no "con," no impression management.

I have learned over time that frequently my mind and my eye do
not see people accurately. My heart is always open, and I believe
that's good. And my gut frequently says, *That person is a human being
and therefore deserving of love.* It also sometimes says, *Don't trust her or
him.* When I am unable to see clearly I don't pay much attention to
my gut. I need to. It never lies to me.

☯

*I am learning to wait with my feelings and information. After all, it's
an insult to trust a person who is not trustworthy. When we do so,
we are not seeing who the other person really is.*

DIFFERENCES/BEING CIVILIZED

Perhaps only when people can enjoy their differences as a re-
source of cultural enrichment do they become truly civilized.
—*Herb Kawainui Kane*
Hawaiian Kupuna and Artist

Differences enrich us. They are not a threat.

Herb Kawainui Kane is a well-known Hawaiian artist. His paint-
ings breathe vigor into a Hawaiian culture that is living and alive
because it is connected to its past. As an artist he is keenly aware of
the elements of cultural enrichment.

His art gives us another chance to appreciate, value, and encourage the vast and enriching differences in our world.

๑๑

*Only when I know who I am can I honor those different from me. Only
when I honor those different from me can I be truly civilized.*

◄O►◄O►◄O►◄O►◄O►◄O►◄O►◄O►◄O►◄O►◄O►◄O►◄O►◄O►◄O►◄O►

RELIGION/FREEDOM/TOLERANCE

Lubaale miliba: buli afuluma alyambala la bubwe.

The idea of God [religion] is like skins: each one [every mortal] will adopt his own.

—Ugandan Proverb

Almost all tribal people believe that the Supreme Being is honored in different ways. Only with Christianity and Islam have I found intense evangelism and the desire to wipe out other religions. In Western thinking, this desire to eradicate differences often seems closely linked with materialism, money, and politics.

If we believe in one God—one basic creative process behind all Creation—why is it so hard to accept God's Creation, including the varieties of peoples and faiths?

The great mystery is so profound that we need as many ways as possible to live the spirit of spirituality.

◉◉

Tolerance is a gift of spirituality. Tolerance is not possible when one believes he or she is the only one who is "right."

CHILD REARING

Childhood among the Australian Aboriginals is the happiest time of their lives. No one who has lived with a group of nomadic hunters, or has spent any time in a camp of Aboriginals who are still living under tribal conditions, can have failed to notice the indulgence and solicitude that is lavished upon the children during their early years.

—*Donald Thompson,* Writer observing Australian Aboriginals

The children are our future. We often hear this, but do we live it?

The Australian Aboriginals can teach us so much about child rearing. They decide when to have children (yes, they have a very sophisticated, ancient form of birth control—very simple—with no drugs) and they have only the number of children their life and environment can support. These children are loved and are lavished with care and affection.

As is the case with Native people the world over, everyone is responsible for the care and loving of each child. The child bonds with the community, not only with its two parents. The child learns from the wealth and knowledge of the entire community. No one can be loving all the time, yet when there are so many people who are loving, the entire environment becomes loving. Also, with so many "keeping an eye out," the environment supports a feeling of freedom and power in each child.

֍

Child rearing is key to a healthy culture, and it is a waste of time to attempt healthy child rearing in a sick system.

SPIRITUALITY

If spirit becomes off balance in the white man's world, they call it sin. Traditional medicine is with the whole being. Most of the sickness today is of the spirit.

—*George Goodstriker,* Kainai (Blackfoot) Elder Canada

Most of the sickness today is of the spirit. To me, this statement says it all. "What does it benefit a people if they gain the world and lose their souls?" A good question.

When we are sick in spirit, our bodies reflect this illness. Yet, treating our bodies alone will never repair our souls.

The Indian people tell us that we will never heal our souls unless we get right with the land, honor our Elders and our ancestors and listen to their wisdom, honor our commitments and treaties, and begin to live our spirituality.

◉◉

Spirituality is the key to our planet's problems. Getting back to spirituality is simple and not easy.

⊷⟨○⟩⊷⟨○⟩⊷⟨○⟩⊷⟨○⟩⊷⟨○⟩⊷⟨○⟩⊷⟨○⟩⊷⟨○⟩⊷⟨○⟩⊷⟨○⟩⊷⟨○⟩⊷

NATURE

See that sea gull? You hardly ever see one anymore. People come here just to shoot the birds—sea gulls, sparrows—there's no sport in that. It doesn't make sense. Now we hardly have any birds.

—Gozotian Fisherman
Malta

Gozo is a beautiful island. It has had many conquerors, and amazingly it has maintained a culture and a simplicity of its own. Only recently has it become a tourist haven.

What kind of people go to a small, simple culture and kill its songbirds for sport? No one eats them.

How sad it is to wake up in the morning, look out over the majestic Gozotian countryside toward the sea, and not hear a single songbird.

This is like the Native Americans' story of the buffalo.

◉

We have so much to learn from nature about living. We and our grandchildren won't learn it if nature is not here.

LEARNING

When you are ready, come to me. I will take you into nature. In nature you will learn everything that you need to know.
> —*Rolling Thunder,* Cherokee Medicine Man
> American Indian

The wisdom of great teachers is that they let their pupils find them. Native Elders need not seek pupils or set up organized classes for teaching. A major task of the student is to seek out and find his or her teacher, and often the process of the search is the true learning. How will we ever find out what we need to learn if someone else is determining what we need to learn? If we are forced to learn a particular skill, how will we know if it is the skill we are here to learn?

Surely, part of our task in this life is to learn what it is we need to learn.

And nature is the classroom for learning about ourselves and our universe. Nature teaches us through all our senses simultaneously and requires that we use our whole brain and our whole being. Knowledge that is abstracted and disembodied from parts of our brains, and unconnected to our beings, may be useful for creating technology, and it will never move us to wisdom. Wisdom asks more of us.

I should seek a wise teacher only when I am ready to learn with my entire being.

MISTAKES/PARTICIPATION

A man begins cutting his wisdom teeth the first time he bites off more than he can chew.

—Irish Saying

Success is not always the best teacher. When we can see our mistakes not as failures but as opportunities for learning, life becomes much, much easier. It is only in a perfectionistic society that mistakes are seen as "bad." It is only in a society based on the illusion of control that people come to believe that by sheer will they can control their lives *and the lives of others* to such an extent that they can prevent mistakes. All systems based on the illusion of control are addictive systems.

Cultures that live in peace *with life* focus on participation with life, not on control.

❧

Wisdom starts with mistakes.

THE TEACHINGS OF OUR ELDERS

Yeah, they [the boats] go in the caves. When I was sixteen years old, I used to fish with a Hawaiian who was born and raised in Kalalau. There was plenty fish in those caves. They'd hide there from the big fish. Now, no more. The sea caves have oil slicks from the boats. The oil just goes out but then it comes right back in.

—*Kaipo Chandler,* Hawaiian Kupuna

Hawaiian fishermen, for the first time ever, are beginning to speak out about what is happening to their rivers, ocean, and other places they consider sacred. It takes a lot for Hawaiians to speak up. It is not a part of their culture to be political or aggressive. Basically, they are a gentle people.

Many Hawaiian families are dependent upon hunting and fishing for the food on their tables. Fishing is not just sport, it is tradition, culture, preserving the old ways, an art, and a way of providing food for their families.

☯

Spending a day with a Native Elder feeds my mind, my soul, my creativity, and my being. I am grateful for all those who preserve the old ways.

WALKING WITH WAKAN-TANKA

Remember and think about the closeness of Wakan-Tanka [the Creator, the Great Spirit]. If they believe in this wisdom, it will give them endless strength and hope.

—*Frank Fools Crow*
Lakota Chief and Spiritual Leader
American Indian

Frank Fools Crow was one of the clearest and most powerful people I have ever known. Never was I in the presence of anyone who consistently walked so close to Wakan-Tanka. His entire life was devoted to treading the spiritual path and healing those who came to him. Just being in his presence was a source of strength and healing, and he shared his knowledge and wisdom with all who came. He never discriminated.

For Fools Crow, Wakan-Tanka was not an abstraction. Wakan-Tanka was a friend, an adviser, an expert, a physician, a colleague, and a constant companion. Wakan-Tanka was a sponsor and mentor. Wakan-Tanka was the boss, always, and one had only to walk the path of Wakan-Tanka and consult with Wakan-Tanka in all one's affairs. And Frank Fools Crow did.

Wakan-Tanka is not an abstraction in our lives. Wakan-Tanka is our lives.

UNKNOWN CORNERS

> I will sing you to safety.
>
> —*Aunt Millie,* Australian Aboriginal Elder
> and Keeper of Sacred Sites

Aunt Millie was ninety-three years old when I met her. Two Aboriginal women of power had taken me to see her at the former mission where she lived. When we got there (after hours of driving), we learned that Aunt Millie wasn't there. She had gone walkabout! I couldn't even fathom what it would mean for a ninety-three-year-old woman to go walkabout.

I was told that Aunt Millie would return soon, as she is the designated Keeper of Sacred Sites in her area and she had to attend to them. Aunt Millie and these sites have a relationship with one another: She is responsible to and for them and must preserve their Dreamtime.

I must confess that while my Western mind did not understand this, my Native being knew that I was in the presence of the sacred when I met Aunt Millie. She is obviously a woman of great power, and much respected by those around her.

She welcomed me with open arms. I tried to believe that it was because I was with these two powerful Aboriginal women, one of whom will take Aunt Millie's place as Keeper of the Sacred Sites when she dies. Yet, I knew that it was *me* Aunt Millie welcomed.

Before I left, she said, "You have much to do. I will sing you to safety." And she did.

❀

Sometimes I forget how much love and protection I have in my life.

CHUTZPAH/ELDERS

On some of the *marae* [the Maori meeting house, grounds, and gathering place], they [the men] have the notion that women should not be allowed to speak. I don't believe that. In Maori culture women have as many rights as men. Everyone should be able to speak, especially the Elders.

I went to a *marae*, and when they said I couldn't speak, I pulled my dress up and pointed down there [crotch] and I said, "Who do you think you are? Where do you think you came from? Every one of you came from a woman. Remember that!"

—Maori Kuia (Elder) and Stateswoman
As told by Dame Whina Cooper

As I sat with and listened to Dame Whina Cooper, I realized that there was no way I could ever convey my gratitude to her for the experience of spending time with her. She is a feisty ninety-six-year-old who has earned the right to say whatever she wants whenever she wants—and she does!

It is not just her words of wisdom that make her so special, it is who she is and the courage she has lived that makes being in her presence a learning in and of itself.

⊚⊚

The older we get, the less we feel the need to please others. That's why it is so important to listen to our Elders.

◄◆►◄◆►◄◆►◄◆►◄◆►◄◆►◄◆►◄◆►◄◆►◄◆►◄◆►◄◆►◄◆►◄◆►◄◆►

FREEDOM

The Irish people are by right a free people.
—The Irish Declaration of Independence, January 21, 1919

We are all a free people. Each of us is born a free person. Free to be ourselves . . . free to practice our spirituality . . . free to practice our culture.

During my childhood, I was periodically reminded that I was Irish. To me being Irish meant: a quick temper that easily spent itself and was not dangerous, a gift for gab, knowing the "little people" and the magic of this world, a family Christmas that included opening presents on Christmas morning. It meant a lot more than that, and I could not articulate it.

I remember deciding, on my first trip "back home" to Ireland, I would travel around and get a "feel" for the homeland of my ancestors. What I experienced was a surprise to me. I felt a fierce sense of love of freedom and justice coming right up out of the earth of my ancestors. There was no energy of conquest or of imposing ourselves on others. There was simply an unspoken legacy of freedom and justice. I realized that my Irishness had given me two of the most important principles that have guided my life.

೫೦

In many lands of the free, the Natives have not been free. Freedom is a right of us all.

KEEPERS OF THE EARTH

A long time ago the Creator came to Turtle island and said to the Red People, "You will be the keepers of the Mother Earth. Among you I will give the wisdom about Nature, about the interconnectedness of all things, about balance and about living in harmony. You Red people will see the secrets of Nature. You will live in hardship and the blessing of this is you will stay close to the Creator. The day will come when you will need to share the secrets with other people of the earth because they will stray from their spiritual ways. The time to start sharing is today.

—*Don Coyhis,* Mohican Writer and Consultant
American Indian

So many Native people the world over are carrying this message. They have kept the secrets of their ancestors and passed them down from generation to generation, and now is the time to speak out. We have, indeed, strayed from spiritual ways. Western mechanistic science is not based upon interconnectedness, harmony, and balance. Rather, it is based upon escape from intimacy and isolation, conflict, and imbalance. There is no place within Western science for spirituality. Native people have a science that is always moving toward the greater and greater—toward the whole. Western science is based upon reductionism—moving to the smaller and smaller, taking apart, isolating, and alienating.

@

Something is happening in the "whole" that has tribal people the world over speaking out with the same message. We need to listen and learn.

HUMILITY/THANKSGIVING

We had been taught by our *Kaumatua* [ancestors] and everything that comes from *Papatuanuku*, the Mother Earth, has to be returned. She has an army of many creatures within her, ready and waiting to recycle and enrich the soil when all is broken down.
—*Mihi Edwards*, Maori Kuia (Elder)

What a wondrous creation this Mother Earth is! She not only feeds us, she breaks down our wastes after us. Rarely do we stop to reverently let ourselves be aware of all the creatures large and small that contribute to our existence—that enhance our existence.

How humbling it is to realize that ultimately we are food for these creatures and that we need them to return us to our Mother, the Earth.

☉

When all things are one, there is no one-up, one-down.

SCIENCE/BALANCE

The earth is out of balance with itself and with the sun. Our legends tell us that there is a flow of energy that goes through the center of the earth and that "rod" keeps it in balance with the sun. If too many minerals and metals are taken out of the earth, it begins to wobble in relation to the sun. If too much is taken out, the earth will be destroyed.

—*Reuben Kelly,* Elder
Thainghetti People, Gurrigan Clan
Koorie [Australian Aboriginal]

Mr. Kelly is the most beautiful man. He was raised on a mission compound where Aboriginal children were taken when they were "removed" from their parents. The boys were trained to do hard labor and the girls to be domestics. Mr. Kelly taught himself to read and write and is extremely well read and knowledgeable in Western ways. Perhaps more important, he is also educated in the ways of his people. He knows their stories, myths, and legends and he uses these to balance and inform Western teachings.

Mr. Kelly's science is profound. His legends, myths, and his ancestors had taught him what our scientists are just beginning to probe and understand. I came away from our meeting feeling that he could easily and quickly have taught me more than I have learned in years of study.

෨෮

Science is not only bigger than we think, it may be much older than we think.

TIME FOR THE CREATOR

The bigger the life the larger the space in that life that should be given to the Creator.

—*The Reverend Akaiko Akana*
Hawaiian Minister and Kupuna

What an interesting idea! The better we do, the more we have, the more successful we are, and the more important we are, the more time and energy we should devote to the Creator.

Imagine what this means! In Western culture, just the opposite seems to be true. The more important we get, the less time we have for the Creator.

೧೪

Making time for the Creator in our daily lives is not a luxury. It is a necessity.

HOW FAST AM I GOING?/HOW MUCH DO I MISS?

If I had to go a long ways I'd use three dogs and then tie them halfway. Go the rest of the way snowshoeing and packing. You know, standing on the sled we don't take in everything. Sometimes we miss the tracks the dogs go so fast. . . . Walking is better. Then we could see every little track that we could find.
—*Madeline Solomon,* Athabaskan Elder
Koyukuk, Alaska

I used to own a big Buick stationwagon that had a 375-horsepower engine. It really zipped over the mountain passes, never losing power. Then I reached a point where I realized I didn't need that kind of power and I bought a Volkswagen camper. We crept over the mountains *and* I saw so much more.

☯

Maybe the reason we need so much is because we're going so fast.

◄○►◄○►◄○►◄○►◄○►◄○►◄○►◄○►◄○►◄○►◄○►◄○►◄○►◄○►◄○►◄○►◄○►

SHARING THE KNOWLEDGE OF THE ELDERS

Christmas trees are cut without prayers. We need to respect Mother Earth and care for the planet.

—*Franklin Kahn,* Navajo Elder
American Indian

Franklin Kahn is a beautiful, gentle, soft-spoken man. Like most Native American Elders, he freely shares his knowledge and wisdom. Franklin comes from a land where there are few trees, and those that are there are highly valued.

The last time I saw him, he spoke with passion and feeling about our treatment of the trees we use for our Christmas festivities. These trees are cut without the proper ritual. They are not asked if they are willing to be cut, they are cut without saying the proper prayers, and no gifts are given to Grandmother Earth for the gift She has given us. For Franklin, this cutting is like murder.

How wonderful it is for those of us who live where trees are plentiful—so much so that we take them for granted—to have someone like Franklin Kahn to remind us that each tree is a sacred gift.

֎

There is so much to learn. We need the Elders from many places and many races to teach us!

PROVERBS

Little dogs make most noise.

—Maori Proverb

Why is it that people who have the least to say often talk the most? Why is it that talking a lot often covers up having little to say?

Native people seem so practical about human nature in their proverbs. There is almost no beating around the bush about who people are and what they will do.

I have often found that the proverbs of a country communicate the wisdom of the culture. The issue, then, becomes how often they are used and the belief in their validity as teaching tools.

☙

The proverbs of a culture are necessary learning tools. We need to use them more often.

CONQUEST

Close packed sounds, intimate and urgent, pattered against the foot of the hills. It was the arrival of the cattle and sheep and the first rush of fugitives. Tirconaill was in smithereens. The noises in the night were the tumbling of a civilisation. The smoke shrouded more than the sky; it was the dead-clothes of a nation. The fires were not merely making ashes of homes, they were making cinders of a people; to-morrow would be sapless as the chores. Tirconaill was no more. Out there in the East careened the victors.

—*Peadar O'Donnell,* Irish Writer

Rarely have I read such an eloquent description of a people and a culture. How fiercely the Irish hold to the concept of freedom, and how vocal they are about the attempts to destroy their culture. Tribal people the world over identify with such attempts to have their culture destroyed.

The Celts, as Daniel Martin said, "adopted rather than colonized, absorbed rather than imposed."

ଚ୨

Jesus said, "The meek shall inherit the earth." Does "the meek" mean people who live with indigenous wisdom?

‹‹◊›‹◊›‹◊›‹◊›‹◊›‹◊›‹◊›‹◊›‹◊›‹◊›‹◊›‹◊›‹◊›‹◊›‹◊›››

THE OLD WAYS

Long time ago people live by these things because that's the only way people can get along. By looking at things the right way. We live close together . . . the way I was brought up has nothing to do with no Whiteman way. Absolutely. What I learned is the Indian way.

—*Peter John*, Athabaskan Elder and Chief
Minto, Alaska

What does it mean to live by what we believe, to look at things the right way? Most of us know the "right" way. We hear it in words in churches. We hear it from family and friends. We even legislate it. Yet, the more laws and punishments we have, the less we seem to *do* things the right way.

I have been so impressed with how Native people such as Peter John *live* their beliefs. They not only talk the talk, they walk the walk.

The key to living a full and healthy life is meaning what you say, saying what you mean, and *doing* it.

ᓄᓇ

Talk is cheap. Cons are easy. Action requires a commitment.

BEING LOVED AND BEING TOUCHED

I flew over from Honolulu to dance for you because I heard you were having a luau at your house and I wanted to be with my family.

—*Reki Chandler,* Young Hawaiian Entertainer

I have known Reki Chandler for a long time. His family and I are *ohana* [family], and to the kids I am Auntie Anne. Reki used to ride his horse on the beach and stop to talk to me every day. We talked about life, horses, education—whatever—and I was his auntie.

Whenever I see any member of the family, I am always smothered with hugs and kisses. Whenever we are together, someone is always touching me and giving me love. Why are so many people afraid of loving and touching?

ෙ

Loving and touching are good medicine for the soul.

MAY

LEISURE TIME AND ATTENTION

Indeed, it is pains-taking attention to each object and each moment that makes possible this self-sustaining culture that nonetheless provides Ladakhis with much leisure time.
—*Helena Norberg-Hodge*
Describing the culture of Ladakh

It wasn't so long ago that our parents and grandparents were told that technology would give us a life of leisure. Why is it, then, that in industrialized nations people have less time for their families, for spirituality, and for vacations (which are often not leisurely!), and for leisure?

Isn't living the process of paying "pains-taking attention to each object and each moment"? Living in the moment is something we have to train (or retrain) ourselves to do.

ॐ

Being present to each moment of my life is living my spirituality.

JOY

O, listen! Hear! Sing with me, for I am joy.

—Cherokee Song
American Indian

I am joy. It's not that I feel joy. I *am* joy. What an affirmation of being!

Too often, I believe, we have been trained to think of past civilizations as less than our own or that the quality of life was inferior to ours because they lacked all the "conveniences" we have today. As I talk to indigenous Elders, I get a very different picture. Of course, there are the younger Native people, who accuse the Elders of romanticizing the old culture. These youngsters feel sure they know more about that culture than do those who experienced it. The Old Ones tell me of living in tune with the earth and the Creator. Of fish and berries and Mother Earth providing. Of knowing their place and knowing that they always have a place. Of family, clan, and community living together.

◍

Being joy is living with the Creator on a moment-to-moment basis.

GENEROSITY

Everyone in my family learned massage. My *tutu* [grandmother] taught me a special kind of massage that belongs to my family. We all know it. I am the only one who practices it now.
—*Alan Alapai*, Hawaiian Kahuna (Healer)

I learned about Alan from the Hawaiian woman who gives me Lomi Lomi (Hawaiian massage). She gets her massages from Alan. One day she was going on about how great Alan is and said to me, "Why don't you let Alan give you a massage? He will come to your home, but let's have him come here and you could steam before and after."

Surprised, as it would "take business away from her," I said, "Are you sure you won't mind?"

She looked at me as if she thought I had blown a circuit and laughingly said, "Of course not! You'll love it! But, be prepared. It's a four- to five-hour massage. You may not want to plan anything for the rest of the day or even the next day."

I did it. I loved it! I am so glad that Alan's grandmother insisted he learn this kind of massage and that my Hawaiian friends are so loving and generous.

In showing a generosity of the soul, we learn the true meaning of abundance.

◄o►◄o►◄o►◄o►◄o►◄o►◄o►◄o►◄o►◄o►◄o►◄o►◄o►◄o►◄o►◄o►

SEEING/HEALING

I'm the spirit's janitor. All I do is wipe the windows a little bit so you can see out for yourself.

—*Godfrey Chips,* Lakota Medicine Man
American Indian

All great healers know that they do not do the healing. In fact, when they believe that they do the healing, they move from being healers to being technicians.

Most real healers know that healing is a process that takes place between a person and his or her Creator or Higher Power.

Sometimes it helps us to have someone "wipe the windows for us." The best window washers know to remove the fog and then stand back.

๑๏

There are so many ways to heal. Arrogance may have a place in technology, but not in healing. I need to get out of my own way if I am to heal.

━◊━◊━◊━◊━◊━◊━◊━◊━◊━◊━◊━◊━◊━◊━◊━◊━◊━

HUMOR

Humor is the WD-40 of healing.
> —*George Goodstriker,* Kainai (Blackfoot) Elder
> Canada

Native people often laugh and joke among themselves, teasing and poking fun at sacred cows. There is an ease and friendliness at being able to laugh at themselves and others.

Wit and humor not only ease life, they lubricate the healing of wounds. Usually, our seriousness about our problems simply feeds them. We often elevate our problems, put them on an altar and worship them, thus making them the most important focus of our lives. Humor cuts our problems down to size so that we can see them in their proper perspective.

❧

Humor reintroduces balance. I need both humor and balance in my life.

BIRTHING

Here is another thing they did. Just before the reddish discharge ['ina 'ina] came, the woman would be given a "birthing" potion to drink [la 'au ho 'ohanau keiki]. Then the kahuna ho 'ohanau keiki would assume the birth pains. The woman carrying the child would not feel the pain, but would just give birth to the child. All she had to do was to prepare herself for the birth, and the contractions and straining of childbirth were assumed [aia maluna] by the kahuna. This is a very difficult thing to do. I have seen kahunas and midwives [po'e pale keiki] who could do this, but they are few and far between.

—*Samuel Manaiakalani Kamakau*
Hawaiian Kupuna

Tribal people possess so much scientific and medical knowledge that we won't allow ourselves to know because it doesn't fit into our scientific paradigm. If the basis of science is open-mindedness, we have failed miserably.

What a wonderful gift for a birthing mother to have someone else bear the pain of childbirth, freeing her to focus on the birthing of her child. What if the father could learn to take on the pain of birthing? What a wonderful possibility for full participation in the bringing of a new life into the world.

◉◉

Closed systems believe that they have nothing to learn from open systems. In fact, they often refuse even to admit the existence of open systems. How much we are missing when we can't see beyond the closed system.

MYSTERY

The mystery offends so the mystery has to be extracted.
                              —*Brian Friel,* Irish Playwright

Western science cannot afford to acknowledge a mystery that it cannot solve. Yet, paradoxically, it is mystery that lets us know our place in the scheme of things. Without mystery, we risk what has become the undoing of modern people. We risk falling prey to the belief that we are God and that we can, indeed, know and understand everything.

It is such a relief to know that we do not have to understand everything—that much of life is mystery.

The Irish are particularly good at mystery. The mists in the hills and the wooded dells invite an awareness of mystery. Perhaps this is why the English tried to burn the woods of Ireland!

❧

Mystery invites belief.

◄◇►◄◇►◄◇►◄◇►◄◇►◄◇►◄◇►◄◇►◄◇►◄◇►◄◇►◄◇►◄◇►◄◇►◄◇►◄◇►

RESPECT

The only way to conquer the *pakeha* [white people] is to marry them.

—*Dame Whina Cooper*
Maori Kuia (Elder) and Stateswoman

There is never a dull moment with Dame Whina, a feisty ninety-six-year-old who has fought for the rights of her people for many years.

Unfortunately, in general, when tribal people have intermarried with whites, there has been a concerted effort to "assimilate" them into Western culture. "Assimilation" has always meant destroying Native people, their culture, and their wisdom one way or another.

Dame Whina is certainly not advocating assimilation. Rather, she is talking about two equal people living their own power bringing the uniqueness of their gifts to the relationship. She is talking about creating something new out of the richness that each contributes to the other. This requires openness, respect, and most of all a recognition that each person is uniquely valuable. (She is also talking about getting their land back!)

๑๑

What would happen if the nations of the world related to one another from an assumption of equality?

BALANCE

We always stop here when we go by. Over four hundred of our people were driven off that cliff to their death—mostly women, children and old people. Sometimes, especially at night, you can hear the weeping, moans, and screaming.

—*Faith* and *Lorraine*
Australian Aboriginal Elders

We stopped, got out of the car, and paused for a few moments of silence. We wept. I wept . . . for a people I did not know personally, and yet I knew their story. I had heard it thousands of times the world over.

The issue is not "Well, they have done that to other people. That has been the history of conquest." (Incidentally, the Australian Aboriginals have *not* "done that to other people.")

The issue is that we as a human family have learned to accept this behavior as human. Only when we feel the grief of what we do to one another will we change. Only when we see that we behave like this when we overtax our natural resources and do not value the richness of the diversity of the world can we begin to plan for diversity and balance.

❦

Only when I see the big picture can I live the small picture.

LEISURE/SERENITY

Then, wherever they stayed, they settled in for winter. And they celebrated—they ate and told stories.

—*Peter Kalifornsky,* Dena'ina Elder
Alaska

Why do we force ourselves to believe that people we call "primitive" have it a lot worse than we do? Would many of us give up modern plumbing to have the whole winter to celebrate, eat, and tell stories? Maybe. Would we give up traveling by jet to live healthy lives well into our hundreds? Maybe.

In order for Western culture to prosper, we have had to convince ourselves that we have it better. In living and being with Native people, I'm not so convinced.

Anthropologists try to convince us that we "romanticize the Native," but then anthropologists have never been known to be big on spirituality.

∞

When I am with Native people, I know that peace and serenity are my birthright.

◆◇◆◇◆◇◆◇◆◇◆◇◆◇◆◇◆◇◆◇◆◇◆◇◆◇◆◇◆◇◆◇◆

THE ELDERS

The old people were never put aside. They were the professors, *te tohunga* of Maori education in all fields.
—*Mihi Edwards,* Maori Kuia (Elder)

When we want to learn a body of academic knowledge, we go to college professors. When we want to learn about *living*, we need to go to those who have done it the longest and learned the most about it.

In a culture that worships high technology, the teachers become younger and younger because we place the greatest value on the latest technological advances. As a result, we are looking more and more to those who have less and less wisdom and are instead relying on "information" to guide our lives.

All Native people value their Elders as the repositories of wisdom, not only about a way of life but also about living our lives.

☙

The wisdom of our Elders is necessary to be able to use information wisely.

RECOGNITION THAT WE DON'T HAVE TO BE ALIKE/ RESPECT FOR ALL RELIGIONS

When he and I were discussing it one day, Black Elk told me he had decided that the Sioux religious way of life was pretty much the same as that of the Christian churches, and there was no reason to change what the Sioux were doing. We could pick up some of the Christian ways and teachings, and just work them in with our own, so in the end both would be better.

—*Frank Fools Crow*
Lakota Medicine Man, Spiritual Leader,
and Chief American Indian

One of the ways to have peace on this planet is to recognize one another's differences and to respect and guard them. Nothing is more supportive of peace than the recognition that all religions are important. What is important is that the spiritual life be lived in a way that is "correct" for every person within her or his culture. We do not need to be the same. Wakan-Tanka (the Creator, the Great Spirit) is mysterious beyond our comprehension. By our very existence each of us adds new dimensions to our understanding of the mystery.

🌀

There are many paths to Wakan-Tanka. Each of us must find our way. My search is enhanced when I value and respect others on their way.

◄0►◄0►◄0►◄0►◄0►◄0►◄0►◄0►◄0►◄0►◄0►◄0►◄0►◄0►◄0►◄0►◄0►

HONOR

I still lived up to my promise and gave him half the fur but he wasn't worth it.

—*Billy McCarthy, Sr.*, Athabaskan Elder
Ruby, Alaska

I hear this time and again in Native cultures in which people operate out of a personal code of honor. Even if they have made a bad agreement, they take responsibility for their commitments. Native people see the harm it does to themselves not to honor their commitments. This then leaves the other person to deal with his lack of honor.

All Native people seem to know that "others can injure my body but only I can injure my soul," and in their cultures it is deemed very important to nurture one's soul.

@

Personal honor is not open to compromise or negotiation.

FRIENDSHIP

"Visi, is that you?"

"Anne, is that you?"—and she fell all over me with great hugs and kisses.

—Samoan Elder

Visi is my Samoan cabdriver in New Zealand. Wanting to find material for this book, I called for a cab one day to take me to some used bookstores to look for unusual old books. At the first stop I expected her to wait and keep the meter running while I ran in. Not Visi. She hopped out and we both rummaged through books. When she found out what I was researching, she began to talk about her life and family in Samoa and offered to introduce me to her family, if I went there. I always call her when I am in town and we visit . . . we visit like old friends . . . we visit like family.

Her bear hugs and kisses remind me how good loving is—not sexual—just good. I love counting Visi as my friend.

@@

Just being with my friend from Samoa opens doors of loving that remain closed in an uptight society where escaping from intimacy is normal behavior. I am grateful for Visi.

SACRED TRUSTS/INTERCONNECTEDNESS

The water feeds the island and the island feeds the people.
—Hawaiian Elder

The old Hawaiians had a very efficient food-production system that fed thousands of people living in a very small area. The taro fields and the fish ponds fed one another, just as the islands, rains, and the sea were interdependent.

The old Hawaiians were very attentive to the needs of the land, of the fish ponds, and of the sea, just as they were aware of the gifts of all three.

Hawaiians see their relationship with the earth and the sea as a sacred trust. They see themselves as stewards of the land and sea. And in return the land and sea both care for them.

When I see the land and the sea as a sacred trust, I interact reverently with them.

BALANCE

A balance does not exist at this time as there is no input by Native people into this world.
—*Douglas Cardinal*
Canadian Indian Architect, Writer, and Artist

What does it really mean to listen to Native people? I see so many people who want to "borrow" their clothes, their art, their rituals, their secrets, their spirituality, and absorb it into Western thinking. But this is not listening to and respecting their input. This is stealing. This is conning.

In order to listen to Native people, it is necessary to see and respect their worldview as viable and necessary. We need to heed this wisdom so that the human race and the planet will continue not only to grow and evolve but to survive!

We can no longer steal to survive. We need to share to evolve.

SEEING IS BELIEVING

Kusikia si kuona.

Hearing is not the same as seeing.

—Swahili Proverb
Tanzania

Often we find ourselves caught in a battle of misperceptions. We are told one thing and experience another. People play with our minds. Some do so deliberately!

We want to believe what we hear. Politics is built on gullibility. But when we listen to this Swahili proverb, we become less gullible, and we ask of ourselves and others, "Practice what you preach."

We need to learn to trust our "gut feelings." We always know when we're being lied to if we just listen to our internal information system. Even when we try to turn it off, it's still there, guiding us to the truth.

✺

Why would I have all this internal information if I'm not supposed to listen to it?

MAY 18

‹o›‹o›‹o›‹o›‹o›‹o›‹o›‹o›‹o›‹o›‹o›‹o›‹o›‹o›‹o›‹o›‹o›

LIVING WITH THE SOURCE

It would have shocked Polingaysi, as it shocked her parents and other Hopis, had she been old enough to understand that the missionaries considered them wicked and unsaved. Their religion was not a Sunday affair; it was a daily, hourly, constant communion with the Source, the Creator from whom came all things that were, large or small, animate or inanimate, the power behind Cloud People, Rain People, the Kachinas, and all the other forces recognized and respected by the Hopi people.

—*Polingaysi Qöyawayma,* Hopi Elder
American Indian
As told to Vada F. Carlson

Only a system that believes it has the right, yea, even the *mandate,* to dominate and control (and often destroy) would have the arrogance to see a people who live every moment of their lives in deep spirituality as "wicked and unsaved." Only a system that has replaced God with its own self-image would lose daily contact with Creation. It is only when we withdraw from the ongoing creative process that we find ourselves estranged and alone. Only then does the ongoing creation become an enemy.

൭൭

When I participate in the ongoing creative process of the universe, I have no time to judge how others participate.

◆◇◆◇◆◇◆◇◆◇◆◇◆◇◆◇◆◇◆◇◆◇◆◇◆◇◆◇◆

ROOTS

Our family was blessed. We had big grandma Kaili 'ohe. Although she taught us not to tell stories "out-of-family," to listen to the boasters and braggers and keep our truths to ourselves, she saw it as very important for our own children to know the truth about who and what they were.

—*Pali Kealohilani Lee*
Paia-Kapela-Willis 'Ohana
Hawaiian Kupuna

How can we know who we are if we don't know our roots? Throughout history we have references to something more than genetic material being passed on from generation to generation, for example—"The sins of the fathers are visited upon the sons." Yet, Western science really recognizes only genetics.

What if there is more? What if we need to know our *kumulipo*, our genealogy, to know *who* we are? Only when we know our true lineage can we place ourselves in historic time and recognize where we are and where we belong. This kind of family understanding does wonders for our self-centered sense of isolation.

ᯤ

When we know our place in the universe, we belong, we have context, we have ourselves.

MESSENGERS

Ehara taku toa i te toa takitahi
Engari takimano, no aku tupuna;
Te mana, te wehi, te tapu me te ihi,
I heke mai ki ahau, no aku tupuna . . .

My greatness comes not from me alone
It derives from a multitude, from my ancestors;
The authority, the awe, the divine, and the artistry,
I inherited these gifts, from my ancestors.
—*Te Maori* Exhibit

Native people have held their secrets and preserved their knowledge, and now it is time to share this knowledge. The world needs this knowledge now. Myths, legends, and prophecies have told Native people that this time would come. I hear variations of this message from Native people the world over.

The above words accompanied the Maori art exhibit *Te Maori* on its trip to the United States. The Maori people ceremoniously gathered their most powerful pieces from all over New Zealand and, despite their pain at letting these treasures leave their homeland, sent them out in hopes that the power of these works could speak to our souls at this time when our planet needs healing. The pieces in the exhibit were not just art. Each is imbued with the knowledge, the power, and the spirit of the ancestors. They felt that experiencing even a part of what this gift means would change our lives.

૭૭

The gifts that are offered to me far surpass my ability to receive them.

◄O►◄O►◄O►◄O►◄O►◄O►◄O►◄O►◄O►◄O►◄O►◄O►◄O►◄O►◄O►◄O►

THE UNSEEN

Well, Elizabeth Anne, it isn't only what you can see that's important. Sometimes it's the unseen that makes the seen worth living.
—*Manilla Maude Longan*
Irish Mother

How can we live our lives so that we are open to the gifts of the unseen?

We want so much to *know*. Yet often it's the honoring of what we don't know that has the greatest influence upon us.

In fact, most of what influences our lives is unknown to us. Do we know when the sun will shine? Not really. Do we know how long our spouse will love us? Not really. Do we know what effect our ancestors have had upon us? Not really.

୭୨

Living comfortably with unseen forces may be our greatest challenge. Letting go of the illusion of control may be our greatest help!

RESPECT

Don't steal, don't lie, don't be lazy. Let's just respect each other.
—Peruvian Woman Speaker

So simple, yet so profound!

Is it stealing to take from others what we don't really need? Is it stealing to convince others that they need something they don't need? Or is it just lying? Is it lying not to know what we really need and so to keep taking more than we really need? Are we being lazy when we expect others to do our work for us, whether the labor is psychological, spiritual, or physical?

If we stop and really explore what it means not to steal, not to lie, and not to be lazy, we can learn a lot. We can begin to see that respect is not something that we can will or demand to occur. Respect emerges as we clean up our own lives.

If I don't steal or lie and I am not lazy, I respect myself. As I come to respect myself, I respect others.

◄◊►◄◊►◄◊►◄◊►◄◊►◄◊►◄◊►◄◊►◄◊►◄◊►◄◊►◄◊►◄◊►◄◊►◄◊►

RESPONSIBILITY/CHOICES

No one needs help to get into trouble.

—Maori Proverb

There are some things I can do by myself. What a relief! I was beginning to think that I had to do everything as part of a community in order to become enlightened!

Of course, if I had the input of those around me who love and care for me, and if I were willing to listen to the wisdom of those who've had much greater life experience, I might not have to learn everything the hard way.

The choice is mine.

☙❧

When I take full responsibility for the choices I make, I may not be willing to make so many foolish choices.

OPEN SYSTEMS

You are always welcome to the circle of my campfire. You are family.

—*Phil Lane, Sr.,* Yankton Lakota Elder
American Indian

When Phil Lane, Sr., said these words to me, I knew that he had checked me out. That he had looked into my heart, and trusted me. *And* even more important, I knew that there would always be room for me around his campfire.

Any system that is built on the illusion of control is a closed system.

Like most Native people I know, Phil lives in an open system. In his worldview there is room for all that the Creator has made. Still, he will not run the risk of destroying his system by welcoming in people whose goal is to destroy his system.

Open systems, by their very nature, allow closed systems to exist. The nature of closed systems is to destroy anything unlike themselves. If open systems do not permit closed systems to exist, they become closed systems themselves! How, then, are open systems to survive? And without them, how is our planet to survive?

❦

Learning about open systems in a closed system is difficult—and not impossible—when we start with our spiritual core.

◄◊►◄◊►◄◊►◄◊►◄◊►◄◊►◄◊►◄◊►◄◊►◄◊►◄◊►◄◊►◄◊►◄◊►◄◊►◄◊►◄◊►

GRATITUDE/SHARED WISDOM

As many contributors to this book attest, the results of these crude attempts to engineer the demise of the Aborigines have been disastrous. The anger and the pain they feel at their treatment and their distrust of the law is justified by their experiences. Even so, what emerges is not bitterness but wisdom, not hatred but patience, not retreat but a desire to share their culture.

—*Derek Fowell,* Australian Writer

So many Native people seem to have become stronger in response to their oppression and even more aware of how important it is to share their wisdom with us.

Often when they look at us, they see dying people in a desert and, with compassion and without condescension, offer us the planetary water of wisdom.

❦

I am learning to be an empty cup so that when fresh water is poured in, I will be able to receive.

◄O►◄O►◄O►◄O►◄O►◄O►◄O►◄O►◄O►◄O►◄O►◄O►◄O►◄O►◄O►◄O►

SCIENTIFIC MYTHS/OPEN-MINDEDNESS

The Australian government wants to mine that mountain. Our legends tell us that a great serpent sleeps in that mountain and if that serpent is loosed, it will destroy the world. We are responsible for that mountain.

—Australian Aboriginal Elder

That mountain is filled with uranium.

I have often been awed by the scientific wisdom in the myths and legends of the Australian Aboriginals. Their understanding of science is very sophisticated and much more akin to the new scientific paradigm than to mechanistic science.

At times, Western mechanistic science appears to me to be a pimple on the time line of our planet that has become infected with pus and is now draining, soon to leave no indication of its existence as a worldview.

◎◎

Open-mindedness is the basis of science. Listening to the ancient myths with an open mind may save the planet and ourselves.

DEFENSIVENESS

She [her mother] always said, when someone be mean or say bad things about us, to let it go, never fight back or defend ourself. We were to be kind to them instead and see only the good things in others.

—*Clara Honea*, Athabaskan Elder
Ruby, Alaska

I have to keep reminding myself that it is none of my business what others say about me or how they see me. I have also learned that when I fight back or defend myself, I need to stop and get back in touch with my spirituality.

There are so many similarities between recovery from addictions and freeing the "white mind." Why is it that addictive substances and Western culture seem so symbiotic?

❀

When I focus upon my own spirituality and beliefs, I don't need to defend myself.

◄◦►◄◦►◄◦►◄◦►◄◦►◄◦►◄◦►◄◦►◄◦►◄◦►◄◦►◄◦►◄◦►◄◦►◄◦►◄◦►

LEARNINGS

A bad thing usually costs a lot.

—Maori Proverb

Sometimes we think we can "get away with" things in this life. Our complex culture tacitly condemns dishonesty, theft, and personal and corporate immorality. Yet complexity often breeds dishonesty, making it somehow okay, at some level, for us to get away with more. But do we ever really get away with anything? Aren't we the ones who really count? Even if we manage to hide our misdeeds from others, we can't hide them from ourselves.

The Maori know that the major factor in doing a "bad" thing is what it does to us. Only when we make amends for whatever we think we've gotten away with can we truly heal and truly be free.

෨෧

Sometimes we have to pay a very high tuition for our learnings.

TRAINING

A thoroughly trained mind, and a broadly cultivated heart are luminous in the soul of the nation.

—*The Reverend Akaiko Akana*
Hawaiian Kupuna

We in the West have done well in training the logical, rational parts of our brains. But training our minds involves more than just parts of the brain.

The mind cannot be trained without the heart and indeed the entire being, and trained brains have difficulty knowing how to be.

Hawaiians can teach us how to "cultivate our heart." A cultivated heart helps our minds know that we benefit from openness and loving. Minds alone do not relate well. We need relationships across cultures if we are to evolve as a species and as a planet.

❦

Minds debate. Hearts relate.

LEARNING FROM NATURE

The power lies in the wisdom and understanding of one's role in the Great Mystery, and in honoring every living thing as a teacher.

—*Jamie Sams* and *David Carson,*
American Indian Writers

We can learn whatever we need in nature because we are part of nature. Human beings are part of Creation. We live by the same laws as all of nature.

We are not the end product of evolution. We are not above nature. It is not our role to dominate, control, rape, and destroy nature. Our role is to participate in nature.

The animals are great teachers. In order to avail ourselves of their wisdom, we have to be around them, we have to participate with them. We have to be willing to be students of those we have been taught are "lesser beings."

෧෨

When we understand that animals have something we need to learn, we have started upon the path to humility.

STINGINESS

Abalirira ekigula enkumbi: taua munne sso oli ddene.

One who counts in a miserly fashion the price of a hoe: does not give his neighbor much maize.

—Ugandan Proverb

Stinginess usually applies to more than one aspect of a person's life. Stinginess is a way of being and affects everything we do. Most people who are stingy with others are stingy with themselves and, perhaps even more importantly, they are stingy with their communities. Indeed, they may not even want to be a part of their community because such groups allow, invite, even require sharing. Stingy people do not help their communities.

Western culture has promoted the breakdown of community. Does it also promote stinginess?

❀

Generosity of the soul shows in all our doings.

JUNE

⊰◦⊱⊰◦⊱⊰◦⊱⊰◦⊱⊰◦⊱⊰◦⊱⊰◦⊱⊰◦⊱⊰◦⊱⊰◦⊱⊰◦⊱⊰◦⊱⊰◦⊱⊰◦⊱⊰◦⊱⊰◦⊱

ACCEPTING THE UNKNOWN

The Dreaming is ongoing. The ancestors created the rocks, waterholes, plants and people and are a continuing presence today. We continue to be one with our ancestors and that oneness gives us the confidence to know the land and the waterholes created in the Dreamtime.

—Australian Aboriginal Elder

I have come to know enough to realize that I know almost nothing about "Dreaming."

What I do know is that whatever it is, it works for the Australian Aboriginals! They have long since demonstrated abilities to find food and water where others cannot. They have been able to change our Western ideas of reality and push us to experience what we considered impossible—how, we don't know. For some Westerners, this has resulted in a drive to know and understand Aboriginal "secrets."

However, getting access to these "secrets" isn't the issue. The real issue is accepting and valuing the Aboriginals' reality and abilities.

ஒ

When I recognize what I don't know or understand, I am opening the door to further knowledge.

ENJOYING LIFE

I enjoyed trapping beaver more than anything else. It's harder work and all that, but I liked it. You've only got one place to set your traps and you're right there. And you're outdoors and your own boss. Period. In town, why, you really got nothing to do. Out there you've got something to do every day.
—*Edgar Kallands,* Athabaskan Elder
Kaltag, Alaska

Can it be that working hard and having a "hard life" is really okay with some people? Can it be that the "luxuries" of life may not add to the quality of life?

When we start living right where we are and with what we have, life takes on a different dimension. It may be the wanting and the trying to be "out there" that detracts from our life, rather than what we have or don't have.

◉◉

Ugly, indeed, is in the eye and the mind *of the beholder.*

RAISING CHILDREN

In general, children were encouraged to explore and use their environment to learn and discover things for themselves. They were told and shown the places declared *tapu* for them, such as dangerous river holes, cliff faces, swamps, reefs, in fact anything that could be far too difficult for them to cope with unless accompanied by adults.

—*Rangimarie Turuki Pere,* Maori Writer

Imagine, children being encouraged to explore! There is such a difference between learning the world through our beings and experience and learning it only through our brains. Exploration helps us feel at home in the world in which we live.

Tapu means "off-limits," but it is not set up as a power struggle. Rather, it is established in cooperation with the child so that the child may grow and expand his or her boundaries while keeping safe.

Western parents of today have a difficult time letting their children explore, when children are being snatched from their own backyards.

֎

Control does not support growth. We need to find ways to give our children freedom and safety.

SPIRIT OF GOD/HOSPITALITY

I asked my grandmother if she knew him. " '*A'ole*," she said. "*He malihini ho'i.*" No, he was a *malihini*. When I asked her why she fed him, she got angry, ordered me to sit on the floor in front of her, and said, "I want you to remember these words for as long as you live, and never forget them: '*A'ole au i hanai aku nei i ke kanaka; aka hanai aku nei au i ka 'uhane a ke Akua i loko ona.*" I was not feeding the man; I was entertaining the spirit of God within him.

—*Nana Veary*, Hawaiian Kupuna

I love these words. I love this story. How different our world might be if we "entertained the spirit of God" within each person.

We often hear these sentiments in Western culture, and some of us even act on these sentiments. In old Hawaiian culture, this recognition of the spirit of God within each person is *practiced* as a way of life. I have experienced the embodiment of this belief many times.

◉◉

When I entertain the "spirit of God" within each person, that spirit glows more brightly, in them and in me!

SPIRITUAL LAWS

Watching my grandmother serve the stranger taught me the basic law of the Hawaiian cosmology: we live in a spiritual universe governed by spiritual laws.

—*Nana Veary*, Hawaiian Kupuna

What does it mean to "live in a spiritual universe governed by spiritual laws"? Does it mean seeing that the universe as governed by the laws of mechanics is not sufficient for living a full life? I believe so.

Spiritual laws transcend national laws. They link us together as planetary citizens who need each other. National and societal laws are usually made to benefit their creators. Spiritual laws benefit all of Creation and cannot be altered by a small segment of that Creation.

Western culture seems to have moved far from spiritual laws. Native people, who have remained closer to these laws, remind us of what these laws are.

My spiritual family can summon me to return to what I know deep within me.

SPIRITUALITY

Like my family, my children, they're all office workers, and they're just tied up, so tense every day. And for a while they fought alcoholism, which is part of all society, any society. The release that my family is finding is going back to the spiritual ways.

—Nez Percé Elder
American Indian

We keep hearing that addictions are spiritual diseases, yet in Western society we keep looking for mechanical causes and cures.

Addictions have not lessened in the United States. It is just that the media have decided that the "phase" of looking at addictions has passed.

This decision has not been accepted in Native communities. Native people are now seeing the connection between Western culture and addictions: that addictions are not only supported by Western culture but *required* so that we can tolerate what we have created.

Throughout the world, I see Native cultures tackling addictions on a community level. Entire communities are realizing that addiction is not just an individual or a family problem. It is a community and a cultural problem, and whole communities and reservations are going into recovery.

◎

A society that requires addiction for its existence is afraid to look at the reasons behind this need.

WEALTH

Status is gained by mobilizing and redistributing wealth, not by hoarding capital.

—*Patricia Kinloch*
Health Services Researcher in Samoa

What a thought! I have heard this idea from several South Pacific communities. Every time I hear it, I realize that I understand this intellectually, but my materialistic Western being screeches to a halt when I try to move beyond the conceptual stage.

Then, as I was writing this, a little song I heard some black children singing in the late sixties sprang into my mind:

> Love gets better if you give it away
> Give it away
> Give it away
> Love gets better if you give it away
> You end up having more.

If this is true for love, then why not for material goods?

SPIRITUAL ADULTHOOD

All life is ceremony. Every act is a ceremony creating a result in our lives. Every ceremony we do always brings results to our lives. If we do bad medicine to others, we do bad medicine to ourselves. If we keep on doing bad ceremonies, we will eventually destroy ourselves. Any time we live out of harmony, we are doing bad ceremonies. Any time we treat anything with disrespect, whether it is another human being or a plant or an animal, we are performing bad ceremonies. These ceremonies not only have an effect on ourselves but will simultaneously affect everything. We need to use our power well, only do good ceremonies.
    —*Don Coyhis,* Mohican Writer and Consultant
    American Indian

Some religions teach us that we are children. As children, we have less responsibility for what we say and do. As adults, we realize that we are responsible for what goes into our bodies and for the words, thoughts, and behaviors that come out of our bodies.

When we hate, resent, focus on punishment, or try to destroy, our lives are out of harmony. We are creating "bad ceremonies."

When we realize that we have the power to work positively with the Creator and put "good ceremonies" into the world, we realize that we have a place and something to contribute.

❦

My life is my possibility. It's up to me to create good ceremonies.

◄O►◄O►◄O►◄O►◄O► ◄O► ◄O► ◄O► ◄O► ◄O► ◄O► ◄O► ◄O► ◄O► ◄O► ◄O► ◄O►

DEATH/HOLISM

Should Hawaii be overrun with lava, if they saw the *no'ailona* [ancestor's spirit] of their own volcanic spirit (Pele) in the fountains of fire, the people had no fear of death . . . it was their own *kama'aina* [people who live there] who surrounded them with fire.

—*Samuel Manaiakalani Kamakau*
Hawaiian Kupuna

Death has a very different meaning in a holistic scientific worldview. When all things are connected and we participate in this connectedness as a part of Creation, we experience no division between the different forms of existence we take. If this lack of division is true for us, it is also true for our ancestors and the spirits. Therefore, we may change form and still exist.

Every Native culture recognizes some sort of continuation of life after the body stops. Western culture is not alone in that. The difference is that we in Western culture have tried to remove ourselves from the created order. This makes our transition one of going from being to not being. When we participate in all of Creation, transition is only that—transition.

☯

Death takes on too much importance when one is not participating in life.

ELDERS

Our legends tell us that we came to this planet on a space ship made of energy. When it hit this atmosphere, it turned to crystal.
—*Reuben Kelly,* Elder
Thainghetti People, Gurrigan Clan
Koorie [Australian Aboriginal]

Mr. Kelly is a lovely man. He taught himself to read and write and is "well educated." As I spoke with him, I began to realize the vastness of his knowledge, because everything he has learned in Western culture has been balanced by Aboriginal legends and myths. He possesses an impressive scientific knowledge.

I loved the way he presented a science that we are only now just beginning to understand as fact. And even with his brilliance and knowledge, when I encouraged him to write about what he knows, he quietly said that he could do so only after consulting with his Elders and getting their approval.

I wonder what would have happened if George B. Peagram had consulted his spiritual Elders before he gave the research on the atom bomb to President Franklin D. Roosevelt? Or if heads of state consulted with nonpolitical spiritual Elders before acting?

@@

When we listen to our Elders and accept their guidance, we have a better chance of making wise decisions.

THE LITTLE PEOPLE

The leprechaun is a very tricky little fellow, usually dressed in a green coat, red cap and knee-breeches, and silver shoe buckles, whom you may sometimes see in the shades of evening, or by moonlight under a bush; and he is generally making or mending a shoe: moreover, like almost all fairies, he would give the world for poteen [an alcoholic brew]. If you catch him and hold him, he will, after a little threatening, show you where treasure is hid, or give you a purse in which you will always find money. But if you once take your eyes off him, he is gone in an instant; and he is very ingenious in devising tricks to induce you to look around.

—*P. W. Joyce,* Irish Writer

I grew up with tales of the "little people." They were under toadstools, living in the trees, popping out behind the bushes! My Irish family knew them and talked of them as one would of relatives.

The world of my childhood was filled with wonder and magic. Enchantment was the order of the day.

Mechanistic science has no place for enchantment. If it can't be measured, it doesn't exist. The problem is, the important things can't be measured.

Perhaps the "little people" can lead me back to my enchanted world.

<◇◇◇◇◇◇◇◇◇◇◇◇◇◇◇◇◇>

FOLLOWING DIRECTIONS/TRUST

Whenever the Creator gives you something, don't hesitate. Grab it.
—Native American Elder

I have always seen myself as a risk taker. I often go where angels fear to tread, and I walk through many doors that have warning signs on them.

Yet, when the Elder told me not to hesitate, I was taken aback. "Maybe I'd better think about this. Maybe I need to weigh all the implications. Maybe I'm not capable or don't have what it takes." I realized how often I do hesitate, especially in spiritual matters. I do not feel ready. I don't feel qualified. I don't know the right way to do it.

◎◎

I need to trust that if the Creator gives me a gift or an assignment, all I have to do is grab it.

◄○►◄○►◄○►◄○►◄○►◄○►◄○►◄○►◄○►◄○►◄○►◄○►◄○►◄○►◄○►◄○►

SCIENCE

When the charter boats first started four years ago, it was not so bad. Now they got fifty boats running three times a day. You don't have time to throw a line before another one comes by. They come fast, too. You can hear them pounding up and down a thousand yards out. Fish hear them, too. Those boats are making all that noise in their houses. So they go away and find somewhere quiet.

—*Kaipo Chandler,* Hawaiian Kupuna

Kaipo doesn't need any scientifically researched data to know what happened to the fish in his waters. In this struggle between tourist boats and the survival of the food source for the local people, the boatmen called for the scientific statistics that would *prove* that the fish were being affected.

The Hawaiians know the fish, they know the waters, and they observed the results. Rarely do Native Hawaiians speak out about the assaults on their food supply, their way of life, and their experience. But this time they have.

The fish are gone. Kaipo's "scientific" evidence is simply his observation: "Those boats are making all that noise in their houses. So they go away and find somewhere quiet."

❧

"Science" comes in many forms.

EASY DECISIONS

When I had that illness [cancer] and I didn't die, I knew that
there was some reason for me to still be around. So I prayed and
thought about it and knew that I was supposed to build a *marae*
[complex of buildings and land for meeting] here on this land of
my ancestors. It's finished now. That's what I needed to do.
                                        —*Uncle Henry,* Banks Peninsula
                                        Maori Elder

Uncle Henry died within a year after telling me this story. He had
taken the last few years of his life to rally his *whanau* [family] to provide a meeting place, a spiritual gathering place, a place to come together for *tangi* [death ceremonies], and a place for eating together.

A *whanau*—an extended family—without a *marae* has lost an important part of its identity. Uncle Henry was giving his *whanau* back
its place before he died.

Once we have been welcomed onto the *marae*, we are always
whanau. We have a place, a people. There is a place to hold meetings and classes. A place to deal with the problems of the community, such as addiction to drugs and alcohol. No one owns the
marae, but all are responsible for it.

Uncle Henry was a great leader. He didn't seem to know it. He
knew only what he must do.

෨

*When I do what I must do, I don't have to spend a lot of time
thinking about whether I should do it or not.*

SAYING FAREWELL

Now the Stickdance is over. We did it. We did what was right. I can sleep good now. You have to talk with my wife about what's behind the Stickdance. She was raised in it and knows all about it. I don't know much, but they say after somebody dies until you have Stickdance it's just like they're wandering around yet. Then they might get lonesome and take their friends with them. We have to do certain things so their spirit can rest. It's lot of work and take lot of money. Now it's over and we did the best we could.

—*Henry Ekada,* Athabaskan/Japanese Elder
Nulato, Alaska

The Stickdance was forbidden for many years. Missionaries told the Native Alaskans that it was evil and that God would not like them to do it. I can't imagine a God who doesn't want every soul to have every possible send-off it can.

As I read Henry Ekada's words, I felt such respect for the openness, sincerity, and gentleness with which he spoke. Surely he has the right to send his dead son to the spirit world however he chooses, and to deal with his grief in a way that is healing for him.

☯

We are all spiritual beings who can learn from one another.

PROVERBS

In Fijian society, one who is able to cite proverbs in their appropriate context at meetings and so forth is looked up to as one who is "wise in the ways of his people." He is talked about and praised for his oratorial ability.

—*Eci Kikau,* Writer
Bau-island, Fiji

I love the proverbs of different cultures. They are always simple yet profound. I find this to be true in Western culture as well, although I think we're using our proverbs less and less today. This means there's a gap in the support we have from the wisdom of our ancestors. In most Native cultures, wisdom, both in the present and from the ancestors, is expressed in the frequent use of proverbs.

To use proverbs often and well demonstrates great wisdom and brings deserved honor. In fact, in some countries, not to know and understand the proverbs makes communication almost impossible because proverbs are the currency of speech.

When my currency is proverbs, I am very rich.

✦◦✦◦✦◦✦◦✦◦✦◦✦◦✦◦✦◦✦◦✦◦✦◦✦◦✦◦✦◦✦◦✦

THE HUMAN FAMILY

O Great Spirit, who made all races, look kindly upon the whole human family, and take away the arrogance and hatred which separates us from our brothers.

—Cherokee Prayer
American Indian

When I hear American Indians pray, I'm always so impressed that they are praying for all of us. In spite of the treatment they have had by the white race, they always pray for us.

Sometimes, I believe, we think abstractly that we are a human family. Unfortunately, abstract thinking rarely results in action. When I *know* I am part of a planetary human family, I will look to the needs of my brothers and sisters, respect the ways of my aunties and uncles.

๛

Wealth is having many relations.

DIVINE LAWS

The rise of *mana* [the power of] Maori is a positive and liberating experience which is part of the international struggle by indigenous populations such as the Maori for self-determination, cultural survival, and escape from domination.

—*Sydney Moko Mead,* Maori Writer

When we view the planet from the perspective of the spiritual laws that rule the universe, it seems unbelievable that our indigenous populations have to struggle to survive. Yet, this is the world we have created.

What a small step it is to see that, just as the planet needs all the many varieties of flora and fauna, we need the voices and wisdom of these Native people.

Only when we see that we need variety for survival will we truly begin to live by spiritual laws.

෨෨

If the Creator created these differences, then they, like we, are governed by divine laws.

◄◦►◄◦►◄◦►◄◦►◄◦►◄◦►◄◦►◄◦►◄◦►◄◦►◄◦►◄◦►◄◦►◄◦►◄◦►◄◦►

HAPPINESS

You mean, everyone isn't as happy as we are?
—*Tsering Dolma,* Ladakhi Farmer

It has been my experience in spending time with Native people, that they generally work very hard and laugh a lot. Humor and laughter flow freely among Native people. When they are with one another, or among people they trust, there is a lack of tension and an ease and a flow that is so peaceful.

Growing up in the South, I often experienced this with my black friends, and as an adult I have missed this cultural happiness.

Unfortunately, I know very few white Westerners who have lived with Native people who have had my experience. In the past, we have been too busy trying to impose our culture to let ourselves experience what we might be missing. I have to admit that being with Native people has always felt to me like "coming home."

◉

No, Tsering Dolma. Everyone isn't as happy as you are.

GREED AND SELFISHNESS

Greed and selfishness are considered serious crimes and are severely punished.

—*Jennifer Isaacs*
Editor, *Australian Dreaming*

Greed and selfishness: These behaviors can destroy a society. In most Native cultures, they are severely punished.

While greed and selfishness are outwardly frowned upon in Western culture, in reality they are tacitly accepted and even admired.

If greed and selfishness can destroy a Native culture, what must they wreak on a much larger scale?

೦೦

I do know one thing. Greed and selfishness will destroy me.

◄○►◄○►◄○►◄○►◄○►◄○►◄○►◄○►◄○►◄○►◄○►◄○►◄○►◄○►◄○►

GREED

In the old days all these Native people were interested in was making a living. They just took what they needed. They knew that if they left fur animals, they were going to be there next year. It was healthy for the animal population that way because they took the older, bigger animals and the new ones could keep coming.

—*Al Wright,* Athabaskan-Anglo Elder
Minto, Alaska

We're just beginning to talk about managing resources, something that every Native population has been doing for centuries. The key is not to take more than we need. Native people have also had a great respect for and relationship with the animal kingdom. Need and greed are not at war in Native cultures. There is a spiritual understanding that greed will destroy.

◎◎

Greed is very costly, spiritually. Can the planet afford it?

WAITING WITH OPEN ANTICIPATION

Their [the Celts] meaning as a people was held more in the cyclic nature of the ongoing story than in the clear cut boundaries of time and space.

—*Mary D'Arcy*, RSM
Irish Writer

What does it mean to operate outside the "clear cut boundaries of time and space"? I don't know . . . and I have a strong feeling in my gut that it means something very important about the way I live my life and what has value in it.

At least I know three things very clearly: It is important that I understand the cyclical nature of the ongoing story; it's important that I know that I don't know what this means; and it's important that I know that I won't find out what this means by trying to figure it out.

☯

We all have something to learn from ongoingness. What is required of us is that we wait with open anticipation.

SIMILARITIES

When I was courting, some of the girls wanted to marry me and told me so, but my father said 'Wait, you'll want to marry every one of them, but some of them have no sense in their heads, let me see them all first and then choose one for you. If you look at them, you'll be taken by the ones with big breasts, and fine big arms and legs. Never mind all that, I'll look out for a girl for you, it doesn't matter if she's small or plain in the face, all that matters is her two hands, I'll find out how she makes gardens and tends pigs. If she doesn't listen to her parents but just thinks of holding up her head and going around courting all the time, she'll be no good.

—*Ongka*
New Guinea "Big-Man"

Sounds familiar, doesn't it? Maybe we need to think we are so different from people we call "primitive" because we can't afford to see that we are so similar.

If I see the similarities between a New Guinea "big-man" and myself, I cannot depend upon differences to keep me safe.

KNOWING OUR PLACE

I teach my children to hunt the old way. When they make the first kill on the hunt they leave all the insides, including the heart and the liver, for our relatives, the winged, the four-legged, and the crawling, and we thank the deer or whatever animal we kill for laying its life down for us so we can live and eat their meat. We say our prayers in unspoken language and respect whatever we kill or dig or pick.

—*Jeanette Timentwa*, Colville Lake Tribe Elder
American Indian

Jeanette is a working Elder. She takes children who are torn by alcoholism and drug addiction (either their own or their family's) and she teaches them the old ways to help them heal. Jeanette tried working in a mental health clinic and decided that "white-man's ways" would not work with "her kids."

Jeanette not only gives these young people something to live for, she gives them a history, a place, a way to know who they are. She teaches them to respect their Elders and how to live in the old ways. She teaches them how important it is on a young person's first hunt to stop and remember her or his place in the created order—a sure cure for self-centeredness and a reminder that every act is sacred.

I feel honored to know and love Jeanette and to participate in her work.

☺◍

When I know my place, I respect the place of others.

LEARNING

Try to understand water, minerals, vegetation, animal behavior, and then it is easy to understand human behavior.
— *George Goodstriker,* Kainai (Blackfoot) Elder
Canada

Our university is all around us. If we are part of Creation, then we can learn what we need to know about ourselves by being in creation and watching, listening, and learning.

What can we learn from watching water? Sometimes when water hits a rock, it splashes hard against it, and then its force is dissipated as it is broken into droplets. And yet, those droplets and their descendants may eventually break the rock up or seek the easier way to go around it.

What can we learn from vegetation? That a plant, in order to grow, needs the earth, the air, the sun, and the water. As these provide for all the plants' needs, so the plants provide for ours.

What can we learn from animals? That they are not judgmental and do not try to analyze one another.

@@

When I understand that humans are just part of the created universe, I have a better understanding of my place.

‹O›‹O›‹O›‹O›‹O›‹O›‹O›‹O›‹O›‹O›‹O›‹O›‹O›‹O›‹O›‹O›‹O›

CHANGE AGENTS

Here [in the Celtic warrior] was no marauding bandit, no simple imperialist. To this day, the Celt has adopted rather than colonized, absorbed rather than imposed.

—*Daniel Martin,* Irish Writer

". . . Adopted rather than colonized, absorbed rather than imposed." These words impressed me. The Irish have not colonized. This certainly does not mean that the Irish have not traveled or migrated to new places. The Irish people are known the world over for their wandering ways, but they never traveled as colonizers. It was really the Irish who saved the art and wisdom of the Western world when Europe was plunged into the Dark Ages. Irish scribes preserved many writings.

Even when the Irish had the upper hand, they absorbed rather than imposed. What does this mean? Of course, we could say, "Well, they never had great armies or navies. They were never a dominant nation." Yet, even though they were known as fighters, they were never conquerors. Historically, they have been warriors of change, not conquerors.

❧

Participating in change is much different from trying to impose it.

INTIMACY AND HEALING

More so perhaps than in Western medicine, the *amchi*'s experience is all-important. His patients are his fellow villagers, so he has an intimate knowledge of their habits and character.
—*Helena Norberg-Hodge*
Writing about Ladakhi culture

Since the Ladakhi healer treats the whole person, and almost always uses a spiritual focus for healing, it is important that the healer know the patient well. Living and working in the same community gives the healer the advantage of the greatest possible knowledge of the patient.

In the Ladakhi culture, healers are not considered gods. They are not elevated socially. Nor do they expect to be. Body, mind, and spirit are all recognized as important parts of the person, working together with one another. Illness is seen as a general imbalance.

֎

In almost all Native cultures, the healer who knows you best is perceived as the one who can best facilitate your healing.

SUFFERING

Suffering is only letting go of things that don't work anymore. On the other side of suffering is belief.

—*Don Coyhis,* Mohican Writer and Consultant
American Indian

We cause ourselves to suffer when we try to hold on to that which is past. The Creator's universe is evolving, and we have the option of participating in that evolution.

We appear to be the only beings in all of Creation who try to stop this ongoing process and make our world static. In so doing, we are attempting to take ourselves out of the Creator's evolving plan and put ourselves above it. Thus, we cease to participate in the ongoing plan of Creation.

It is not surprising that our attempts to make the world static and to separate ourselves from the creative process, and thus from the Creator, brings us only loneliness and suffering.

@>

Belief is participation. Spirituality is participation. Only when we participate are we in touch with the spiritual.

⊷⟨◦⟩⊷⟨◦⟩⊷⟨◦⟩⊷⟨◦⟩⊷⟨◦⟩⊷⟨◦⟩⊷⟨◦⟩⊷⟨◦⟩⊷⟨◦⟩⊷⟨◦⟩⊷⟨◦⟩⊷⟨◦⟩⊷⟨◦⟩⊷

MY PLACE TO STAND

This is my place to stand.

—Maori Saying

I had made many trips to New Zealand and had spent many days with my Maori friends and my *whanau* (family) before I even began to have some understanding of what is meant by "This is my place to stand." I know that I have still more to learn about its meaning.

"My place to stand" means that I belong. I have a *whanau*. I have a tribe. I have a land. And because of those connections, my feet are rooted firmly in the earth of my ancestors and I have my place. I am not confused about who or what I am. I know. I have the blood of my ancestors surging through my veins, and no one can take this identity from me.

So many Maori have expressed their observation that the *pakeha* (white people) seem ungrounded and that even though they have "their" land in New Zealand, they have "no place to stand" because they do not have the connection with their ancestors.

◉

"My place to stand" may be far more important in my life than it seemed at first.

ALOHA

Every race was put on this earth for a reason. The Hawaiians were for sharing the true essence of aloha—love for everyone and everything.

—*The Reverend Akaiko Akana*
Hawaiian Kupuna

This has been my experience! My Hawaiian family and friends have taught me more about loving than I had ever believed possible. They know how to do aloha. In Western culture, I am often perceived as a very loving, giving person, and I believe I am. Yet, I find my "white mind" playing tricks on me when I am with my Hawaiian friends.

For example, some of my friends invited me over for dinner, a salt scrub, and music. However, I also knew they were charging fifty-five dollars for these soirees, which they held every weekend. I found myself running through a series of mental gymnastics about going. I loved my friends and wanted to support them. But I didn't like the caterer much. I loved Hawaiian music. I could steam anytime I wanted to for free, since I had contributed to the building of the steam room. It went on and on. I finally decided that the fifty-five dollars was a contribution to my friends and not a fee for services rendered, and I felt fine about that, especially since I would be spending time with people I love. I arrived, ate, steamed, and was lovingly salt-scrubbed . . . only to be informed that I was their guest. They wanted to give me this treat.

Open hearts have a way of soothing closed minds.

JULY

SEVEN GENERATIONS

Look behind you. See your sons and your daughters. They are your future. Look farther and see your sons' and daughters' children and their children's children even unto the seventh generation. That's the way we were taught. Think about it—you yourself are a seventh generation.

—*Leon Shenandoah,* Onondagan Elder
American Indian

Everything I think, everything I feel, and everything I do affects the generations that follow. How different my life would be if it were guided by this awareness!

I make decisions every day. That is part of the privilege and responsibility of being human. In making decisions as an adult, it behooves me to be ready to accept the consequences of my decisions. And I am not the only one who has to accept the consequences of my decisions. My family, my friends, my community, my country, my planet, and those who follow me must also accept the consequences of my decisions. Somehow, in modern society, we have been able to isolate ourselves to such an extent that we believe that what we decide and what we do doesn't even affect us! It does, though, and it affects those who come after us.

❀

I ask the Great Spirit to give me knowledge and awareness so that the choices I make will honor the Creator and serve the generations that follow.

HONORING OUR BODIES

The best thing for your body is making love with a righteous partner every day. The next best thing is Lomi Lomi [Hawaiian massage], the next best is belly dancing.

—*Auntie Margaret*, Hawaiian Kuhuna

Because we were raised in a society that is obsessed with sex, it is difficult to imagine what it would be like not to sexualize our bodies or our relationships and only just to live with them naturally.

As Shakespeare said, "Nothing is either good or bad but thinking makes it so." What have we done with our thinking about our bodies in Western culture? Our bodies are just that—our bodies. The Creator did not give us something to live in that is "bad." We have added that element to our belief system. It is very difficult to find people who are "sexually clear" in our society, and we have spread that lack of clarity throughout the world.

☯

God has given us many gifts, one of which is our bodies.

FREEDOM

Believe we too love freedom and desire it. To us it is more desirable than anything in the world. If you strike us down now we shall rise again and renew the fight. You cannot conquer Ireland; you cannot extinguish the Irish passion for freedom; if our deed has not been sufficient to win freedom then our children will win it by a better deed.

> —*P. H. Pearse,* Irish Leader of the Easter Rising, speaking to the court-martial that sentenced him to death (1916)

Freedom of the soul. Freedom of the spirit. Freedom to use one's own language, to practice the customs of one's culture. Freedom to live as descendants of one's ancestors. This is the freedom that most tribal people ask.

Freedom does not mean freedom to dominate or to impose our ways and beliefs on others. Freedom is the right to make the unique contribution that each of us and our people can offer to the evolving planet on which we all live.

☯

Freedom is the right to exercise diversity and live our truth.

◄◦►◄◦►◄◦►◄◦►◄◦►◄◦►◄◦►◄◦►◄◦►◄◦►◄◦►◄◦►◄◦►◄◦►◄◦►◄◦►◄◦►

PEACE AND SIMPLICITY

I'm just glad that now the sun does rise and the days are warm, so that I can listen to the birds singing happily, and the animals munching away at their food.

—*David Gulpilil*
Australian Aboriginal Actor and Writer

I had such a feeling of peace as I read this statement—peace and simplicity. A lot more could be said . . . a lot more *has* been said . . . and why? Sometimes, all we need is to get back to gratitude for the basics and let life take it from there.

೧൦

When I get too busy to stop and be grateful, I probably need to re-examine my priorities.

BELIEF SYSTEMS

Failure to appreciate the importance of indigenous belief and practice lies behind the limited success of various Western health interventions in the Third World.

—*Cluny* and *La'avasa Macpherson*
Samoan Writers

The Samoans have a very sophisticated medical practice not based upon Western beliefs or concepts. Allopathic medicine does not dominate Samoan healing practices. This gives them a perspective of Western medical practices that Westerners cannot have.

Studying Samoan medicine helps us perceive that our Western medicine is built upon a belief system peculiar to our thinking. One that is not shared with much of the world.

In Samoan culture, illness almost always has a spiritual component and can be related to tension in the village or community. The healer has to have a broad knowledge of the seen and the unseen to know the proper treatment. All levels of reality are important in Samoan healing.

@◎

To understand the belief system in which I live, it helps to have the perspective of another system.

❖◦❖◦❖◦❖◦❖◦❖◦❖◦❖◦❖◦❖◦❖◦❖◦❖◦❖◦❖◦❖◦❖◦❖

ROOM TO BREATHE

[About the city of Seattle] But gee, when I look down [from the Space Needle] all I see is just confused like scrap heap. And you know, at home we have lots of mosquitoes summertime but at least they have room to fly between one another. Here it's like there are more people than our mosquitoes!

—*Madeline Solomon*, Athabaskan Elder
Koyukuk, Alaska

Sometimes it's difficult for us "civilized" people of the world to believe that "primitive" people such as Madeline Solomon can look at our way of life with all its advantages and not want it. It's even more difficult to believe that they find our way of life not only undesirable but primitive.

Human beings need space to be human. We need air, sunshine, good water, and contact with nature. Without nature, we are displaced persons.

❦

When Native people say what they think, it sometimes rocks our reality.

A LOVING GOD

The Elders teach us that the Creator is a loving and forgiving God. He loves us during our good days and he loves us during our bad days. He doesn't know how to do anything but love. If I really want to find out about the true God, I only need to ask in prayer. There is one thing that God cannot do and that is refuse help to one of his children who asks.

—*Don Coyhis,* Mohican Writer and Consultant
American Indian

How has our belief in a spiteful, punishing, guilt-evoking God affected who we have become as a people? Or is it vice versa? Why, in the entire history of this planet, have we given such weight to a theology that is only a speck on the time line of the planet?

Native American Elders teach of a God that is more in keeping with my experience. I am the one who gets me in trouble, and it is usually when I move away from what I know to be the true ways of the Creator. It has never been that God has left me. I am always the one who leaves.

And, when I ask, return is always possible.

When I ask only to do the work of the Creator, the Creator responds.

RELATIONSHIP TO THE LAND

The rhythm of the land and the rhythm of his blood had been one and the same. And he had begun the planting and both blood and land had gradually become calm.

—*Witi Ihimaera*, Maori Writer

Witi Ihimaera writes beautifully about being Maori and the Maori people. His books augment my experience of being with his people.

In the passage above, he is talking about an old man who knows that he must go out and renew his relationship with the land. This is a living relationship . . . a mutual relationship. The land is not calm until he comes back into relationship with it. He is not calm until he comes back into relationship with the land. As they reestablish their relationship with each other, both are calmed.

This is not a relationship of dominance and rape. This is a relationship of mutual need and respect.

❦

We have much in our lives, and some things are missing. I am drawn to those who teach me about the rhythm of the land and the rhythm of my blood.

NATURE

Begin to care for nature and nature cares for you, in unsuspected ways.

—*Bill Neidjie,* Australian Aboriginal

What's the payoff? What if we begin to care for nature and nothing happens? How can we learn how to care for nature anyway?

An Australian Aboriginal—and most other Native people, for that matter—would never ask these questions. In fact, these questions would never even occur to them.

They would just start.

How often our questions keep us from starting! How often the need to know the outcome prevents us from beginning! In these ways, we miss the unexpected experiences of life's journey.

֍

Our need to know keeps us from learning so much.

BEING "IN" THE WORLD

You're calming down enough to be in your world.
—*Nani,* Hawaiian Kupuna

How important it is to be "in" my world. Of course, it is probably not possible to be in my world if I am not "in" myself. I have to stop, wait, listen, and calm down in order even to begin to be in myself. In fact, almost everything in my culture invites me to *leave* myself, to drug myself and thus dull my awareness of what my body is telling me. Even more, my society invites, even demands, me to be out of touch with the world around me and my living environment. What would happen if I let myself feel the noise, hear the pollution, and smell the violence around me? I have to be "numbed out" to take the world we have created.

Yet, when I retreat, get out in nature, and calm down, I can be in my world. And when I am in my world, I know deep within my soul that we must cease to destroy it.

֍

Being in my world lets my world into me.

LOST KNOWLEDGE

I give the young people lot of chance to learn what I know and yet nobody take it up. Free for the asking. Nobody wants it. So that's the reason I let everything drop. Everything going to die with me when I die.

—*Peter John,* Athabaskan Elder and Chief
Minto, Alaska

I have heard this the world over. So many of the Elders are deciding to take their secrets and knowledge with them when they die because they believe that no one wants to learn from them and that there are no people qualified to teach and carry on the ancient knowledge.

What a loss!

Others, however, are saying that their Elders' myths and legends have told them that a time would come when the world would need their knowledge to save the planet. Many believe that time is now.

෧෨

Please, Elders, don't be silent now!

<><><><><><><><><><><><><><><><><><><>

CONTENTMENT

Embugo ziwooma ntono: nga yeebikka bbiri, nga yeesiga ezo okumumala.

Even a few barkcloths can make one happy: if one who covers himself with two is content with them.

—Ugandan Proverb

It doesn't matter how much we have if we are content with it. *And*, it doesn't matter how much we have if we are not content with it. The feeling of contentment is within us. Whenever we look outside ourselves and believe that "something," "anything," can make us content, we have missed the point.

Often, we look upon some who have less material wealth than we do and we say to ourselves, "They are poor." But they are poor from our perspective. We often do not know what makes others contented.

☯

Being "poor in spirit" is what makes me discontent, not the lack of material things.

‹O›‹O›‹O›‹O›‹O›‹O›‹O›‹O›‹O›‹O›‹O›‹O›‹O›‹O›‹O›‹O›‹O›

SACRED NATURE

Nature is the storehouse of potential life of future generations and is sacred.

—*Audrey Shenandoah,* Onondagan Writer

The time has come when we can no longer ignore what we are doing to Mother Earth. Mother Earth is the source of all life. Everything on the planet has a purpose and is necessary for that purpose. When we interrupt the flow of nature, we destroy the planet, not only for ourselves but for those who will come after us. We need to love and respect all of nature. We need to learn to live within the laws of nature, not above them. In nature, we have the assurance of support and protection for generations to come. We are blessed.

၆၇

When I respect all of Creation, I benefit, as I am part of Creation.

◄◊►◄◊►◄◊►◄◊►◄◊►◄◊►◄◊►◄◊►◄◊►◄◊►◄◊►◄◊►◄◊►◄◊►◄◊►◄◊►◄◊►

AROHA/LOVE

Aroha in a person is an all-encompassing quality of goodness, expressed by love for people, land, birds and animals, fish, and all living things. A person who has *aroha* for another expresses genuine concern towards them and acts with their welfare in mind, no matter what their state of health or wealth. It is the act of love that adds quality and meaning to life.

—*Cleve Barlow,* Maori Writer

Maori society is based on *aroha*. There are and always have been warriors, and the quality that is most valued by this society is *aroha*.

Gentleness and loving in men, women, children, and the elderly form the cornerstone of this society. Being loving and gentle in no way takes away from the strength of the Maori.

Love is a word that has become very confused in Western society. In order to feel *aroha*, one must recognize that people are not the center of the universe and that all life is interconnected.

🌀

Aroha *is a way of being, not a way of doing.*

◅◈►◅◈►◅◈►◅◈►◅◈►◅◈►◅◈►◅◈►◅◈►◅◈►◅◈►◅◈►◅◈►◅◈►

EVERYTHING IN ITS TIME

I ran a small Naturopathic clinic out of my very small home in Guatemala. Things seemed to be going too slowly. Grains that we ordered had not come in. The rebuilding of the *Temescal*, a Native adobe sweat lodge, was taking forever. Dov was learning to crawl and it seemed impossible to keep him away from undesirable crawly creatures on the ground, like fire ants. I was feeling frustrated. Señor Castro, his load upon his back, walked down the dirt path at the border of our land and in his inimitably intuitive, sensitive, and "right on" way, he greeted me with the usual *"Buenas tardes, Doctora."* I responded, *"Buenas tardes, Señor Castro."* Then, without skipping a beat, he looked at me compassionately and said, *"Doctora, todo en su tiempo, recuerdas, todo en su tiempo."* ("Everything in its time, remember, everything in its time.")
   —*Señor Castro*, Guatemalan Indian
       As told to me by Latifa Amdur, L.Ac, Dipl. Ac., and C.H.

I need to remember that it is not good to eat fruit until it is ripe, nor is it good to bring forth an unripened idea.

When I try to interfere with "God's time," I am out of sync with myself and everything around me.

Señor Castro, in all his wisdom, knew how to live *with* the world, not against it.

❀

Everything in its time, remember, everything in its time.

HUMOR

If he has a purple countenance and no humor, leave him to the priests.

—Irish saying

Ah, the humor of the Irish! Their wit can teach us much about quick thinking and hard truths.

My mother always said that we have a gift for the gab and a quick wit "because we're Irish."

I have never met a people more ready to laugh at themselves or more willing to tease one another without malice than the Irish. In many ways, people who are without humor are "dead" to themselves and have only yet the formality of being buried.

❀

Humor is life's leavening. Without it, our souls don't rise.

OPEN SPIRITUALITY

God takes care. I don't care whose god it is.
—*Naoni*, Kupuna La'paau

Most Native people "don't care whose God it is." In fact, most Native people are open to everyone's God. They eagerly believe that they have much to learn from anyone who is spiritual and in touch with the spiritual realm. Theirs is an open spiritual system.

An open spiritual system recognizes that there is one God and Creator of us all and that each of us has groped as best we can to understand a mystery that is bigger than all of us.

Most Native people believe that we have a better possibility of coming to know the Creator of us all if we share our searchings.

∞

We need as broad a spiritual base as possible if we are to live spiritual lives.

◄◎►◄◎►◄◎►◄◎►◄◎►◄◎►◄◎►◄◎►◄◎►◄◎►◄◎►◄◎►◄◎►◄◎►◄◎►◄◎►◄◎►

RESPECT

We need to have respect and love for all things and for all people.
— *Don Coyhis,* Mohican Writer and Consultant
American Indian

To live in peace requires a level of respect that is almost foreign to us in this modern world. We want to *make* peace happen. We look with horror at the wars raging among our brothers and sisters around the globe and we feel helpless in the face of the immensity of the task.

Still, the only thing we can really change is ourselves. Respect begins at home. Do I respect my body? Do I give it what it needs and not what it doesn't need? Do I respect the rights and boundaries of others and treat our differences with respect?

Do I respect the Creator's planet and try to walk softly on it, taking only what I need and respecting its ways? Do I try to live in harmony with my Creator and do the work the Creator has for me?

◉◉

Respect is the key to living.

RELATIONSHIP WITH OUR SURROUNDINGS

When asked to compare living today with the old ways, Peter says, "It's hard both ways." The old ways were physically hazardous and dominated by the quest for food, but they were rich in that the people understood their relationship to their surroundings. Their concept of community included land and animals as well as human beings.

—*Peter Kalifornsky,* Dena'ina Elder
Alaska

"The people understood their relationship to their surroundings." This phrase leaped out at me. It is difficult to understand our relationship to our surroundings when we make every attempt in our lives to pretend that we have none. Between our climate-controlled homes, offices, and shopping malls, we have ceased to see any value in relating to the natural world. We find it inconvenient, undesirable. In our attempt to remove ourselves from the created order, we have made a world so contaminated that we don't want to relate to it. Which is the chicken and which is the egg?

◉

When I have no relation to my surroundings, I kill my surroundings and they kill me.

OUR PATH

Everyone has to find the right path. You can't see it so it's hard to find. No one can show you. Each person has to find the path by himself.

—*Charlie Knight,* Ute Elder
American Indian

We have to do it ourselves. We don't have to do it alone. Sometimes we get confused about this. We forget that we are spiritual beings who are one with the Creator. We forget that whenever we call upon the Great Spirit, we always have a companion to travel with us, even though we still have to take the initiative and do it ourselves.

Also, we sometimes forget that in order to walk our paths, we have to be willing to go inside. We have everything that we need to heal inside us. Our healing is in conjunction with the Great Spirit. No one else knows what is right for us.

There is a right path for each of us. We have to be willing to listen to the stillness to hear the directions.

Often, on a moonless night when I need to get from one place to another in nature and I have no flashlight, I know there's a path although I can't see it. I have discovered that if I just stand and wait, the path will emerge. I won't see it. I'll just know it. If I am impatient and I just push on, I will lose my way altogether. Life is something like this.

TRUTH

Kweli iliyo uchungu si uwongo ulio mtamu.

An unpleasing truth is better than a pleasing falsehood.
—Swahili Proverb

Sometimes we think we can't handle the truth and would rather not hear it. We kid ourselves into thinking that a little white lie won't matter. And it does. It hurts us. Dishonesty is expensive. It erodes the soul.

Although we may hurt from the truth for a while and we may even get angry, the truth is never destructive.

Dishonesty is always ultimately destructive, even when it is something we want to hear.

Being lulled with pleasant falsehoods is verbal drugging. Eventually it destroys.

◄O►◄O►◄O►◄O►◄O►◄O►◄O►◄O►◄O►◄O►◄O►◄O►◄O►◄O►◄O►◄O►

HEALTH

Out here our only security was the never-failing cycle of morning
dawn and setting sun. It amazed me that the world's most insecure race, according to my standards, suffered no ulcers, hyper-
tension, or cardiovascular disease.
                    —*Marlo Morgan*
                    From a story about the Australian Aboriginal

What a simple observation! Everything that is supposed to provide security in our culture is lacking, yet here are a people who
suffer none of the illnesses that our security is supposed to prevent.

The whole concept of security is so Western. Security is an attempt to try to make the universe static so that we feel safe.

Instead of trying to learn to live with a universe that is evolving
and changing, and developing skills to do that more effectively, we
have tried to stop the evolution and make life static. No wonder
this stresses the body!

◎◎

Healthy people live with *their world.*

◄◦►◄◦►◄◦►◄◦►◄◦►◄◦►◄◦►◄◦►◄◦►◄◦►◄◦►◄◦►◄◦►◄◦►◄◦►◄◦►◄◦►

CHANGING TIMES

Mirembe gye giseguza.

Times bring changes.

—Ugandan Proverb

Remembering that times bring changes is a good way to mark the middle of the year. As human beings, our time on this planet has been relatively short. As participants in Western culture, our time has been even shorter.

The only constant is change, and we need to develop skills to live with and to participate in change. So many of the skills we have developed have been to try to make our world static. When we are static and controlling, we are not living.

By participating in our own change we can be a part of the changing process around us. Changing times invite us to develop our spirituality, for only our spirituality gives us security in changing times.

&

Changing times are invitations for participation.

SELF-IMPORTANCE

When a thing is funny, search it for a hidden truth.
—*George Bernard Shaw*
Irish Writer

Many times I have found myself laughing and my brain saying, "Wait a minute. There's something more than meets the eye here." Many times my parents pointed out something to me that I didn't want to hear and made it interesting with a twinkling eye, a sly grin, or a loving tease.

I often find myself laughing with tears in my eyes as I experience a great truth carried on the back of humor. Some of the greatness of Irish writers is their ability to see the everyday humor in profundity.

❡❡

When I find I am not laughing very much, I am probably getting too serious about how important I think I am.

THINKING

For every problem solved by the mind, it creates ten more. We need to get to the heart or soul!
—*Phil Lane, Sr.,* Yankton Lakota Elder
American Indian

Many years ago, a thought occurred to me that I like so much: "Decisions have to be discovered." They cannot be made. We can make the little ones, and the big ones have to be discovered.

I believe this statement is related to what Phil Lane, Sr., is saying here. Life—especially the important parts—often is not rational and logical. Logical thinking may be good for a certain mechanical realm of problem solving, but the "big ones" have to be solved some other way.

When my thinking is not balanced by my heart and soul, I get into a heap of trouble.

◂◉▸◂◉▸◂◉▸◂◉▸◂◉▸◂◉▸◂◉▸◂◉▸◂◉▸◂◉▸◂◉▸◂◉▸◂◉▸◂◉▸◂◉▸◂◉▸◂◉▸

CLEANSING

Disease starts in the mind and ends up in the *na'au* [guts]. That's why everyone needs to clean out the *na'au*. Then, the mind clears.

—*Angeline Locey*
Hawaiian Kupuna and Healer

The Hawaiians believe in cleansing—inside and out. There is great respect for the body, and they know that when the body is properly cared for, the whole being is clearer and healthier.

The Hawaiian cleansing as Angeline practices it consists of ten days of fasting and flushing out with seawater. This is a time for resting and giving both body and soul a chance to clean out and renew. She uses gentle Hawaiian foods and Hawaiian herbal remedies for the cleansing. In addition, the diluted seawater flush not only cleans out the body but, when it is combined with a daily sea salt and Hawaiian-clay scrub in steam, "returns ninety-eight trace minerals to the body." All this is done with *aloha* [love].

꩜

Care enough for myself to cleanse my mind and guts. This is something I need in my life.

CHILDCARE/COMMUNITY

But caring for the baby was not her job alone. Everyone looked after him. Someone was always there to kiss and cuddle him. Men and women alike adore little children, and even the teenage boys from next door were not embarrassed to be seen cooing over little Angchuk or rocking him to sleep with a lullaby.
—*Helena Norberg-Hodge*
Describing child rearing among the Ladakh

There are so many advantages of community living! What ever made us think that two parents were enough?

Think what happens to a new being who always has "someone there to kiss and cuddle him." I spend most of my time in community living these days and there are children of all ages among us. My grandson lives in another state, and although we see each other as much as possible, I rarely have long periods just to be with him. I have much more time with the children in my international community. From an early age, we have much contact and they look up and smile when they hear my voice. These children are loved, held, and cuddled all the time by their extended family members.

☯

Children need lots of mothers, fathers, aunties, uncles, and grandparents. This arrangement is good for everyone.

◄O►◄O►◄O►◄O►◄O►◄O►◄O►◄O►◄O►◄O►◄O►◄O►◄O►◄O►◄O►◄O►

WARNING

So they said we must have a meeting. We must start with a prayer, offer it to Mother Earth and Father Sun and to the four directions. Call on all the forces to direct us because from now on we will have to face many problems.

—*Thomas Banyacya,* Hopi Elder
American Indian

I hear this so often from Native people. The Elders are sending messengers (often reluctant ones, such as Thomas Banyacya) to inform Western culture of the meaning of their warning prophecies. Prophecies are not foreign to modern culture. We have a history of them in our religious heritage. However, I do find it curious that Native people, who until quite recently had no contact with outsiders, are the ones being called to make their knowledge and ancient prophecies known to the world.

We try to categorize these concerns as ecological. This means that since we "know" about ecological issues—pollution, the hole in the ozone layer, toxic wastes, and so on—we can turn the problem over to scientists, then continue to behave as we have been.

My perception is that the ecological crisis is only a symptom of the global spiritual crisis that our Native family is trying to call to our attention.

೦೨

It won't hurt to listen.

HARMONY

How can people say one skin is colored when each has its own coloration? What should it matter that one bowl is dark and the other pale, if each is of good design and serves its purpose well? We who are clay blended by the Master Potter come from the kiln of Creation in many hues.

—*Polingaysi Qöyawayma (Elizabeth Q. White)*
Potter and Hopi Elder
American Indian

What arrogance to judge people by the color of their skin, and to assume that the Creator finds only one hue beautiful!

Everything in Creation teaches us that the Creator is an artist who delights in a display of limitless hue, infinite color, and design. If we look at Creation closely, we can experience creativity beyond our imaginations, and a celestial sense of humor. We lose so much when we try to limit the Creator to our own imagination.

෮෮

I am the only real limit placed upon me.

◅◈▻◅◈▻◅◈▻◅◈▻◅◈▻◅◈▻◅◈▻◅◈▻◅◈▻◅◈▻◅◈▻◅◈▻◅◈▻◅◈▻

EDUCATION

The university of ancient Hawaiki is the universe, and as such, education has no boundaries.

—*Rangimarie Turuki Pere,* Maori Writer

In Maori circles, one does not get an education or get educated. Education has no boundaries.

Education is not just learning a technology—that's easy. Education is about participating in the universe and learning as we participate.

When our minds are free to roam the universe, we need not be bound by an allegiance to any particular worldview or belief system.

While we need to know the history and beliefs of our people to ground us, we also need to know that the universal university calls us beyond our rigid boundaries.

೦Ѳ

Education is much more than learning a body of knowledge. It is living wisdom.

THINGS UNSEEN

How much we miss when we don't know the presence of things unseen.

—*Nani*, Hawaiian Kupuna

Sometimes our world is so small, especially when we limit it to our five senses. This deprivation is like turning a richly hued Technicolor epic into a black-and-white movie.

The Hawaiians, and many other Native people, live in a world richly inhabited by things unseen.

How much we have had to reduce our world to rid it of things unseen! How controlling of our experience.

I find that because of my training and background in science, I am not skilled in things unseen. I do not like to be unskilled, yet I sense that I have much to learn about the vastness of my universe, if I will only open my mind and being.

@

I sense that the most important forces in my life are things unseen—such as God.

AUGUST

◄O►◄O►◄O►◄O►◄O►◄O►◄O►◄O►◄O►◄O►◄O►◄O►◄O►◄O►◄O►◄O►◄O►◄O►◄O►

OPENING TO KNOWLEDGE

We have a mountain called White Buffalo Mountain. We called it White Bull Mountain for a long time because we were not allowed to be educated and we did not know about buffalo. When we learned about the American Indians, we knew that the proper name for the mountain was White Buffalo Mountain. It belongs to the American Indians. When the continents were pulled apart, it was pulled down here, but it belongs to the Native Americans.
—Australian Aboriginal Elder

I was impressed with the stories about this mountain. Clearly, it is an important sacred site. It was one of the places that my Australian Aboriginal friends insisted I see.

As we drove to a place where we could view it, I told them about my American Indian friend, grandfather, and mentor who had died the year before. I shared how much I missed him.

"Ah, this mountain belongs to the American Indians. His soul will come here. It isn't here yet and it should be here by the time you return. We'll do a ceremony for him," they said. I was much comforted by their words.

෨෧

There's so much we don't know.

LETTING GO AND SEEING

"We'll take you to see White Buffalo Mountain. A lot of people don't see the Buffalo . . . but we know you will."
—*Hope* and *Lorraine*
Australian Aboriginal Elders

Well, talk about putting pressure on me! Hope and Lorraine made it clear by what they said and what they *didn't* say that only people who are spiritual, who are gifted with special powers, and also are "special" people, could "see" the buffalo. I had spent a lifetime on that dualism—being "special" and not being "special" (nobody), and here it was again. I thought I had resolved this issue by learning just to be who I am, and here these two were giving me another chance to get off the dualism.

Doesn't being special mean that you have to do special things and take on special responsibilities? Who wants to be "special"?

We stopped and got out of the car, and there across the valley was a big mountain and white cliffs with mists drifting across its face. I had worked myself into a tizzy by this time. I looked—I saw white cliffs—disappointment; relief. Now they won't want to spend time with me. Oh, well.

Then I looked up again—and jumped back. A buffalo was coming out of the mountain toward me. I looked at my Aboriginal friends—they smiled. My white friends who were with me asked me to show them where it was. I couldn't. It was a different way of seeing.

❦

Sometimes, what we learn from Native people is how to be ourselves.

TRUE WEALTH

Our greatest wealth is in the number of kupunas (elders) and children.

—*Alex Pua,* Hawaiian Kupuna

How does a culture behave that sees its greatest assets as its Elders and children?

In Hawaiian culture, Kupunas (Elders) are listened to. When a Kupuna dies, it is more than the loss of that person; the whole community is losing a repository of wisdom, culture, and information that they need. The "wealth" of the entire community is diminished when a Kupuna dies, for Kupuna wealth is not the kind of wealth that is replaceable. Unless the knowledge, wisdom, ceremonies, and stories are passed on, an entire society loses pieces of its heritage. It loses pieces of its "story." Only the Kupunas are the living storehouses of who we are.

Then there are the children, the *kamali'i*. The children are our future. The children are the ongoingness of the culture and the living savings accounts who capitalize on how we have spent our lives and the decisions we have made. They will outlive the consequences of our decisions.

☯

Let's put our money where our wealth is.

WARNING

I translate the teaching and compare it with other religions. A lot
of them know the same things Hopi Elders know: we're going to
have big problems in the world. We are children of Mother Earth
and we were sent different areas to take care of, to use our language, our ceremonies, whatever we develop to help keep this
land life in balance. We have no business going around disturbing
other people's land and life. We can help them with every invention we have, but not use that to try and control them.

—*Thomas Banyacya*, Hopi Elder
American Indian

Thomas Banyacya has been chosen by the Hopi Elders to carry this
message to the world. He is just one of the many Native messengers
bringing the warning—to alert and to share—not to control.

He presents an interesting idea to our modern world: that each
area of the earth has the people it needs to care for it. That no one
has the right to move in on another people's land and life and disturb them. That we have a responsibility to care for what we have.

What does this mean for colonialism, conquest, and exploration?
What is the difference between sharing what we have and letting it
go, and trying to control others and make them be like us?

🌀

*The message is clear. It is coming from all parts of the world. What
does it mean for our lives?*

PARTNERS WITH GOD

The Okanagan word for ourselves is *sqilw*. Which in a literal translation means, "the dream in the spiral." We recognize our individual lives as the continuance of human dreams. We know our lives to be the tools of the *vast* human dream mind which is continuing on into the future.

—*Jeannette Armstrong,* Canadian Indian Writer

If our lives are "the tools of the *vast* human dream mind which is continuing on into the future," what does this mean in terms of how we live our lives?

Sometimes, I think we as a human race are still in childhood. We do not want to take the responsibility for being partners with God in creating the future of life on this planet.

We are being given the opportunity to "grow up," to become adult as a species, to not blame others for our lives. We can take a more active role instead of expecting God to do it all. We have the opportunity to be a part of and to help shape that "vast human dream mind which is continuing into the future."

๏๏

If I want to participate in creating the future, I must be willing to give up my attachment to being a victim and take responsibility for being an adult of my species.

◅O▻◅O▻◅O▻◅O▻◅O▻◅O▻◅O▻◅O▻◅O▻◅O▻◅O▻◅O▻◅O▻◅O▻◅O▻◅O▻◅O▻

WELCOMING A CHILD

It is nearly 70 years ago. Dusty roads, furrowed by wagon wheels, overlay the narrow footpaths of old. Frame cottages replace Hawai'i's grass houses. From the roadways, men and women are converging on one of the little cottages. They are all members of the same *'ohana*. They, like their ancestors before them, are gathering to help in an important family occasion. Later, others will arrive to join the celebratory feasting. The event, now imminent, is *hanau*. Childbirth.

—*Mary Kawena Pukui*
Hawaiian Cultural Authority

What a support for the mother, the father, and the new baby! Upon arrival, the baby becomes a part of a community of aloha. Childbirth is not sterile, mechanical, isolated, and governed by technology.

Childbirth need not be lonely. I have been a part of these occasions, and life is affirmed and celebrated every minute.

☙❧

We in Western culture frequently come together for funerals. It is equally important to join together in the bringing of new life into the world.

CHILDBIRTH

Before the appointed back support took up her station, the *pale keiki* [midwife] and family members, often on both sides, had already begun to function as a kind of "obstetric team." The team was concerned, not only with safe delivery of a healthy child, but with the emotional support of the mother in labor, and the psychic focus that could aid or injure mother and child.

—*Mary Kawena Pukui*
Hawaiian Cultural Authority

The above description is used to help Hawaiians remember their culture and their old ways, and to help those who work with them to understand Hawaiian culture.

In Hawaiian culture, it takes a team of people to deliver a happy, healthy, and safe child. Delivery is a group effort, and the mechanics of it are only a small part of the entire birthing process. There is tremendous emotional support for the mother and for the baby.

Perhaps the most important aspect is that there are family members present who know how to take care of and deal with the unseen forces.

When unseen forces are ignored, we miss a big part of the picture.

WORK

A bit of hard work never harmed any man.

—Irish Proverb

I have always been suspicious of anyone who doesn't know how to work. When I reached adulthood, having grown up in a poor family, I was greatly surprised to learn that there were people who actually do not know how to work.

It's not just that people are lazy—truly, some are. There are just some people who don't know how to pitch in and *just do it* when something needs to be done.

I have also discovered over time that people who don't know how to work can't be trusted. I don't know what the correlation is, *and* it's certainly there.

A bit of hard work contributes to the honesty of a person. I can trust people who know how to pitch in and help.

FUN TOGETHERNESS

We Maori display a great spirit of togetherness. If you want proof of that statement, try to hold a quiet party for just a few friends; arrange a sneak departure overseas; or have a quiet fiftieth birthday. I can tell you—you've got your work cut out.
—*Dame Te Atairangikaahu,* Maori Kuia (Elder)

I rarely see a Maori leaving for overseas who hasn't precipitated a family gathering. The sense of community, fun, and togetherness is everywhere.

I was recently visiting at a *marae* [a gathering place where, once one is called onto the *marae*, one is always welcome] that is a "love" *marae* for me. I was sitting and talking with a couple of people in the kitchen. I had arrived unannounced and had decided to stay awhile. Of course I was welcome!

A few minutes later, more people arrived. "I heard you were here" . . . hugs and nose touching, sharing the breath of life. Then, just a little later, even more people arrived—having heard I was there. Then the food started appearing.

☺

I like togetherness. It's difficult to be lonely when we come together.

COMPASSION

Tashi would remind me that knowledge and understanding were not sufficient in themselves. In fact they could be dangerous, he would say, if not accompanied by compassion.

—Helena Norberg-Hodge
Writing about Ladakhi wisdom

Knowledge and information are never enough. No one ever healed from understanding. We can understand absolutely everything about a situation and that doesn't heal the situation. In our technological, information-oriented society, we have been lulled into thinking that if we just have all the information and understanding about what is happening, we have everything we need. Even wars have made us media addicts. Our insatiable quest for information (or misinformation) keeps us glued to our television set for hours, days, weeks.

Where is compassion? Every now and then we try to insert a human-interest story and hope that this can be construed as compassion. Yet, deep in our souls, we feel farther and farther removed from the skills that balance knowledge with compassion.

Knowledge, information, and understanding are *dangerous without compassion.*

LISTENING

Did you know that trees talk? Well, they do. They talk to each other, and they'll talk to you if you listen. . . . I have learned a lot from trees: sometimes about the weather, sometimes about animals, sometimes about the Great Spirit.

—*Tatanga Mani (Walking Buffalo),* Stoney Tribe
Canadian Indian

How rude I have been! As a child, I was taught to listen when I was spoken to. Yet, it seems to me that I often have walked away when the trees were talking to me.

I am ignorant of their language. Yet, I usually do not walk away when someone speaks to me in a foreign language.

Like any language, it takes time to learn the language of the trees. I have Native friends who can help me learn it. I would like to know what the trees can teach me, especially about the Great Spirit.

Just because I can't hear something, that doesn't mean it's not "talking."

GIVE AWAY

Sometimes he [Goodwin's father] did get a black bear in the fall. The fat was about couple inches thick on the back. We always put that away for special time like New Year's canvas toss. People come around shaking a canvas in front of your door and you throw in some food. Then they take it all to the community center and potlatch it out to people. They cut the bear fat into strips because it was very valuable. That's just about the richest food there was for falltime.

—*Goodwin Semaken, Sr.*, Inupiat/Koyukon Elder
Kaltag, Alaska

I've heard this many times in Native cultures: "We saved the most valuable to give away." These people place a high value on sharing and giving away. If something is especially valuable, then that is always what is given away. There is no reason to store up and hoard.

The other thing I hear is that giving has no strings attached. When something is given, there are no expectations (which, in our culture, become premeditated resentments). Since giving is a cultural norm among Native people, what is given always comes back in some form.

☯

Life is circular.

EDUCATION/SPIRITUALITY

The determination that all State schools may not teach spiritual or religious issues, is a direct contradiction for all Polynesian people brought up in a culture system that promotes and emphasises a leadership of man by forces beyond himself. The fear that one religion might outstrip the other or that people will be drilled in one dimensional concept, does not exist in Maoridom. People are permitted and encouraged to accept the reality of a God, and to take part in any series of *karakia* [prayer] that might be in progress. The certainty to the Maori, is that Tane, the giver of Life, has given life to all people and to all things, and following upon this gift of life, all activities performed by people will be subject to spiritual influences.

—*Hiwi Tauroa*, Maori

Only when we have a religion that is a closed system that cannot tolerate the existence of other systems do we have to legislate controls.

Closed systems are by nature controlling and are threatened by open systems. Open systems are not threatened by closed systems because all are allowed existence.

When we legislate our spirituality, our children do not have the opportunity to learn that they are part of the universe, that they and all things have been given life by a Creator, and that there is something bigger than themselves.

ᓚ

Spirituality is easy. It's religions that cause problems.

UNITY/ELDERS

We Lakotas have a term, *Okolakiciye*. When translated to English, it means a league, fellowship, community, or society, without which, unity cannot thrive. In looking at life, we realize the brevity. Life is like the breath of a buffalo in the winter time. So what does that tell us? "Live with purpose and concern for the people. It's brief, my friends!"

—Phil Lane, Sr., Yankton Lakota Elder
American Indian

Phil Lane, Sr., is one of the Council of Elders for the American Indian Science and Engineering Society. He and others like him add their wisdom to the organization and its deliberations. Just their presence gives a grounding—especially a spiritual grounding—to the organization. Their words are wise and their presence is healing.

Often we have to sit with what the Elders say to us and let it ripen within us. At first, what they say may seem not to apply, and then it starts to germinate.

We are blessed to have Elders among us. What might happen if we listened to them?

FEAR/RACISM

... the rugby player and surfie who, suffering from fear of his own inadequacies as a male, believed the racist myth of black virility, and who was now trying to convince himself (and his friends) that the myth wasn't true. The whole history of the *pakeha* [white people] had been cursed with this fear, and the Maoris and other minority groups had to pay for it.
—*Albert Wendt,* Samoan Writer

What have we done to ourselves and others with the "racist myth of black virility"? What have we done to the men and the women of all races with these myths? What have we all done to ourselves?

Many believe that we try to kill in others what we fear in ourselves. And yet, as we face our fears, we have less need to project them onto others. Going into our fears and processing through them will lead us to places of clarity we have never imagined. And, we will not need the other to project upon.

❦

The "-isms" are outgrowths of fear and the refusal to face ourselves.

COMMUNICATION

"Oh, be quiet, crow. We hear you."

"That old crow is a messenger. He's telling us where to go to find Aunt Millie. He's leading the way."

—*Lorraine*, Aboriginal Elder

On this trip, we were supposed to meet with Aunt Millie, a ninety-three-year-old Aboriginal Elder and Keeper of Sacred Sites. But we weren't sure where Aunt Millie was.

I have to say there *was* a crow wherever we stopped, and it was noisy. I did not know the language of the crow and my companions seemed to. Who knows, I thought, he may speak only the language of the Australian Aboriginal. That's not it, though, because my Native friends the world over tell me that the crow is a messenger.

Animals seem to speak a universal language. Maybe if we understood and spoke the language of the animals, we wouldn't have to translate for humans. Australian Aboriginals say that if we have nothing to hide, all of us can communicate telepathically.

We found Aunt Millie.

◉

When I learn to listen to nature, I am never lost.

VISION/HUMANITY/SPIRITUALITY

Now I claim for Irish literature, at its best, these excellences: a clearer than Greek vision, a more generous than Greek humanity, a deeper than Greek spirituality. And I claim that Irish literature has never lost these excellences: that they are of the essence of Irish Nature and are characteristic of modern Irish folk poetry even as they are of ancient Irish epic and medieval Irish hymns.

—*P. H. Pearse,* Irish Writer

It's interesting that Pearse contrasts Irish writing to the Greek, which has basically formed the basis of the Western culture.

A clearer vision—vision gives us the possibility of becoming, of changing, and of evolving. Without vision we become "secure" in stasis.

A more generous humanity—generosity in our humanity helps us to rise to our potential and look to the possibility of being fully human and not clinging to the limiting functioning of reptilian or mammalian brains.

A deep spirituality—the possibility of participating in the oneness of Creation, of taking our place, of knowing our interconnectedness.

☙❧

A clearer vision, a more generous humanity, and a deeper spirituality. Who could ask for anything more?

‹o›‹o›‹o›‹o›‹o›‹o›‹o›‹o›‹o›‹o›‹o›‹o›‹o›‹o›‹o›‹o›‹o›‹o›

MEDITATION

There's many ways to meditate. Some of us go to the mountains, some go beside a river, some go on a hill. There are many places to be by yourself a little bit, to get away from the noisy world. Give yourself a chance.

—*Horace Axtell,* Nez Percé Elder
American Indian

Horace is a quiet man, a strong man. He speaks with humility and power. I like being near him.

I have noticed that the more time I spend with Native people, the more I am drawn to have time alone to "meditate" in the way I find best for me. For me, being in nature is a meditation and I need it for my sanity.

My way may not be another person's way. That's not important. What is important is that each of us finds places of quietude that give us the healing balm of "awayness."

◎

As we find our way to meditation, we give ourselves a chance.

BLESSINGS OF THE ELDERS

I'm a Christian first and then a Hawaiian because I belong to the Kingdom of God.

—*Helena Maka Santos,* Hawaiian Kupuna

As I was writing this book, I learned that Auntie Helena Maka Santos had died at sixty-one years of age. I burst into tears. Another great Kupuna of the Hawaiian people had left us.

Auntie Helena was my friend. She played a mean ukulele, danced beautifully, sang the old Hawaiian songs, and accepted everybody as belonging to the Kingdom of God. She patiently corrected my Hawaiian and helped us all to know that there was much, much more to the Hawaiian language than missionary Hawaiian.

Auntie Helena was a religious person who practiced her spirituality every minute of her life—and shared it freely with every person in her life.

Aloha knew its meaning in Auntie Helena. And humor and laughter, teasing and love, dancing and honesty were what she taught all of us.

☺

Let us help each of us remember how blessed we are to have Kupunas (Elders) in our life.

CHILD REARING

The purity with which the child comes into the world is protected for eight days. Our customs say that the newborn baby should be alone with his mother in a special place for eight days, without any of her other children. Her only visitors are the people who bring her food. This is the baby's period of integration into the family; he very slowly becomes a member of it.

—*Rigoberta Menchú*
Quiché Indian, Guatemala

How wonderful! Although this mother has had to work unbelievably hard throughout her pregnancy, she also has special care throughout, and everyone participates in looking after her health and that of the baby. After the birth, their customs dictate, she has nothing to do but be with the child for eight days with no one else around—she doesn't even have to cook! Such wealth! Such luxury!

What an opportunity for the child to move into the world at its own pace. This certainly gives the child a start in life and a bonding that soon will be spread to the family and the entire community.

֎

Eight days of quiet. That's more than some of us get in a lifetime.

⬦⬦⬦⬦⬦⬦⬦⬦⬦⬦⬦⬦⬦⬦⬦⬦⬦

SOMETHING TO THINK ABOUT

Maybe that's why Valerie never woke up to life yet, she's been around old people ever since she was born.

—*Lorraine Honea,* Athabaskan Elder
Ruby, Alaska

I have noticed this expression—"woke up to life"—a lot in listening to Native Alaskan people. I don't quite know what it means, and I have the feeling that it means something important to the Athabaskan people in Alaska.

Since this expression seemed important for me to ponder, I thought it might be important for others.

☙

Pondering is a good thing.

‹O›‹O›‹O›‹O›‹O›‹O›‹O›‹O›‹O›‹O›‹O›‹O›‹O›‹O›‹O›‹O›‹O›‹O›

POSSESSIONS

The love of possessions is a disease among them.
—*Tatanka Yotanka (Sitting Bull)*
Hunkpapa Teton Sioux
American Indian

How owned are we by our possessions? We talk about materialism as a curse of the Western world, yet I think we often fail to see the implications of materialism. In a scientific worldview that believes that the only reality is what we can grasp with our senses, the material world takes on a very exaggerated importance. In fact, it becomes *all* important because it is the *only* reality. But since the material world does not feed the spirit, we continue to grab for more and more. As we lose the riches of the unseen, we have less and less.

☙❧

Sitting Bull was right. Materialism is a disease among us, and it is killing us.

◄◎►◄◎►◄◎►◄◎►◄◎►◄◎►◄◎►◄◎►◄◎►◄◎►◄◎►◄◎►◄◎►◄◎►◄◎►◄◎►◄◎►

HONESTY

U limi hauna monfipo.

The Tongue has no bone.

—Swahili Proverb

There is nothing stable or reliable about the tongue. It is easy for people to lie, and a tongue can wag about however it pleases.

When we are trained to trust what people tell us, we have very few skills for discernment. It is easy to find oneself in a dualism of trusting everything everybody says or trusting nothing anyone says. Either way, we lose.

When we live in a culture that does not teach us to discern, we are at a loss. Our most effective way of discerning whether we are being lied to is to be in touch with our feelings. Our solar plexus can always give us the information we need, if we will just listen.

෴

It is our responsibility to be realistic and to know whose tongue can be trusted.

EVOLUTION

Civilization is still on the road from intolerance to tolerance.
—*Dame Te Atairangikaahu*
Maori Kuia (Elder)

How wise the Maori are! They recognize that, hopefully, we humans and the civilizations we have created are still on a path of evolution. We have not arrived yet!

Intolerance is a static state, and not a normal state for the human organism. The normal state for any part of Creation is to grow and change. We try to make our world static only when we feel insecure and believe that security comes from stasis. How boring a static universe would be.

In Western culture, we have tried to develop technology and tools to make our lives and our universe static. We need to learn how to teach ourselves and our children the skills necessary to participate in an evolving universe.

❦

Tolerance will allow us to participate in change, and participating in change will give us tolerance.

◄O►◄O►◄O►◄O►◄O►◄O►◄O►◄O►◄O►◄O►◄O►◄O►◄O►◄O►◄O►◄O►

PROPHECY

We knew this is the wealthiest part of this continent, because here the Great Spirit lives. We knew that the White Man will search for the things that look good to him, that he will use many good ideas in order to obtain his heart's desire, and we knew that if he had strayed from the Great Spirit he would use *any* means to get what he wants. These things we were warned to watch, and we today know that those prophecies were true because we can see how many new and selfish ideas and plans are being put before us. We know that if we accept these things we will lose our land and give up our very lives.

—*Dan Katchongva*, Hopi
American Indian

It is chilling to read the prophecies about Western culture that were given long before we came to this country. How does it feel to be called a people who have "strayed from the Great Spirit"? It's difficult to get back to the Great Spirit when our very religions seem to be complicit in the cultural straying. Have we, as a people, strayed from God? Can we be trusted? Are our plans selfish?

☯

If the shoe fits, should I wear it—or look for new shoes? Maybe it's time to go shopping!

◄◊►◄◊►◄◊►◄◊►◄◊►◄◊►◄◊►◄◊►◄◊►◄◊►◄◊►◄◊►◄◊►◄◊►◄◊►◄◊►

WAITING WITH/LISTENING TO NATURE

It took us a long time to decide where the trees and plants belong. After we had finished the *marae* [place of meeting and spirituality], we had all these trees and plants and we were not clear where they belonged. We waited for a long time because it is important for everything to be in its right place on a *marae*. We waited for the plants to let us know where they belonged. One day, I came for the hill and looked down on the *marae*. I could see every plant in its place. Then we could plant them.

—*Uncle Henry,* Maori Elder

I love the way Uncle Henry told this story. As is typical of Maori Elders, he was doing a great deal of teaching in sharing a simple story.

On the surface, he was just sharing what he had been doing. At a much deeper level, he was giving us some profound information. That's the way it is with Elders.

Uncle Henry was teaching us how important it is to do things in their right time. To "wait with" until things ripen. To listen to nature, which is one of our greatest teachers.

❡❡

Waiting with can be important with Elders too—and it's worth it.

BLIND INTOLERANCE/OPPORTUNITIES MISSED

Priests always used to say things against the medicine people. They said don't believe in them. I guess that's the reason I didn't pay much attention to medicine. I went to Catechism every chance I got so I went along with the priests. But I know that there's something to medicine people. I know.

—*Josephine Roberts,* Athabaskan Elder
Tanana, Alaska

Medicine people have powers that are often not understood or controlled by mechanistic science. So just like the women who were healers in the Middle Ages, they are often considered a threat. There are many kinds of medicine people in Alaskan Indian society. There are healers, there are those who can tell the future, those who predict the weather, and those who know the unknown—to name only a few.

These people have a gift that belongs to the community. Usually, they didn't ask for it, and often they were hesitant about accepting it. Yet, they have it. There is no "licensing" to cloak the real from the unreal ones. Their "licensing" is in what they do. If they are good, everyone knows it. If not, everyone knows it.

❧

How can we learn anything if we try to destroy everything we don't understand?

DEVELOPING OUR "ETERNAL BEINGNESS"

It seems Mutants [white people] have something in their life called gravy. They know truth but it is buried under thickening and spices of convenience, materialism, insecurity, and fear. They also have something in their lives called frosting. It seems to represent that they spend almost all the seconds of their existence in doing superficial, artificial, temporary, pleasant tasting, nice appearing projects and spend very few actual seconds of their lives developing their eternal beingness.

—Voice of an Australian Aboriginal
As recorded by Marlo Morgan

A powerful statement! These and other Native people have politely kept their own council for a long time. Now that they have decided to speak out, their words are powerful and to the point.

We use convenience, materialism, insecurity, and fear as drugs to dull our awareness of what we need to see.

How many people in Western culture wake up one day and say, "This is all meaningless," and walk off their jobs forever? More than we realize.

☺☺

What am I doing in my life to "develop my eternal beingness"?

THE FAIRY-FAITH

We now pass directly to West Ireland, in many ways our most important field, and where of all places in the Celtic world the Fairy-Faith is vigorously alive.

—*W. Y. Evans-Wentz*
Writer of Irish Lore

The above was written by Evans-Wentz in the early part of the twentieth century, when he was doing research about the Fairy-Faith in Celtic countries and cultures. The beauty of this classic work is that he has recorded interviews of Celtic people's own experiences with fairies.

I, too, have spent time in western Ireland, and though few there would define themselves as Celts, the Fairy-Faith still creeps in and is still alive and well. My mother always gave a nod to "the little people," and the early residents of the Findhorn community spoke of the importance of the wood nymphs and plant and earth fairies to the raising of their crops.

I do know that there are enchanted glens in western Ireland that invite magic.

❧

By disenchanting our world we have lost something precious.

CHILDBIRTH

The last painless birth was when my older sister was born. In the next room was a lazy relative. A healthy, able-bodied man. Just lazy. While others helped with the birth, he just lay in bed. My uncle, the *kahuna pale keiki*, just prayed to Haumea, the goddess of birth. Then he directed the pain to that lazy brother-in-law of his. The poor fellow began to moan and groan. He moaned until after my sister arrived. My mother felt no pain at all!

—*Mary Kawena Pukui*
Hawaiian Cultural Authority

I love the humor.

I have heard from many Hawaiians that the old Kuhunas knew how to remove the pain from childbirth. They would either take it on themselves or, as in this case, give it to someone else.

How many of us would gladly have taken on all the birthing pain to give our child some relief? I know I would have.

Probably even more important than taking on the pain was that it could be done and was done.

◉◑

There are so many mysteries.

SOFT HEARTS

The old Lakota was wise. He knew that man's heart away from nature becomes hard.

—*Standing Bear,* Lakota Sioux
American Indian

I believe this to be true. For many years I have pondered what must become of people living in cities away from nature. How can we be concerned for the planet when we really have no connection with the planet? How can we be concerned about nature if we never see nature?

We need opportunities for nature to soften us up. We need to reestablish our oneness with nature, and it is difficult to do that when nature seems so removed. An abstract nature is not very workable.

❧

I want a soft heart.

SEPTEMBER

CELEBRATION

The great sea
Has sent me adrift
It moves me
As the weed in a great river
Earth and the great weather
Move me
Have carried me away
And move my inward parts with joy.
—*Uvavnuk,* Eskimo Woman Shaman

How simple it is to celebrate life and the gifts of life in everything we do! Celebration need not be saved for "special occasions." We have the possibility of living life as a celebration.

As I sit and listen to the crickets and the flies buzzing, I have the opportunity to be grateful for their presence in my life and their role in Creation.

As the moon shows its sliver of a new self, I have the possibility of celebrating the lighting of the darkness and the pulling of the unseen forces of the tides.

As I sit down to eat, I have the opportunity to celebrate the bounty of the earth and its generosity with me.

The Creator gives us all so much each and every day.

I celebrate!

SPIRITUAL SECURITY

They do us no good. If they are not useful to the white people and do them no good, why do they send them among the Indians? If they are useful to the white people and do them good, why do they not keep them at home? They [the white men] are surely bad enough to need the labor of everyone who can make them better. These men [the missionaries] know we do not understand their religion. We cannot read their book—they tell us different stories about what it contains, and we believe they make the book talk to suit themselves. If we had no money, no land and no country to be cheated out of, these black coats would not trouble themselves about our good hereafter. The Great Spirit will not punish us for what we do not know.

—*Red Jacket,* Seneca Orator
American Indian

I love the humor, the candidness, the perspective, and the logic of this passage. Red Jacket was eloquent and irrefutable. Most of all, I love the last line: "The Great Spirit will not punish us for what we do not know." This statement reveals such a close, daily, and secure relationship with the Great Spirit that one can rest at ease in that relationship.

❧

To be at ease with the Great Spirit means that I accept the most profound relationship in my life.

TANGI/FUNERAL

The voice of the *tangi* [funeral] has curled across the land. A member of the *Whanau* [family] has gone, and the breaking apart is so profound that the sudden emptiness is felt in every heart.
—*Witi Ihimaera,* Maori Writer

The *tangi* in Maori culture is much more than a funeral. It is held on the home *marae* [meeting place] and everybody comes. It is a time of mourning and grieving as only a *whanau* [extended family] can do. And it is much more.

The voice of the *tangi* is the collected voice of a people loving, honoring, grieving, and releasing one of their own. As we lose the Old Ones, we know that we have none to take their place because fewer and fewer remember a world that knew another way. So the loss of an Old One means not only the passing of a person, it means the passing of a possibility, a possibility of knowing another way. This is a breaking apart so profound that only our hearts can know it.

We need to listen to our Elders before it is too late.

TIME

When you work for the Creator, you go back in nature. You work in "his" time.

—*George Goodstriker,* Kainai (Blackfoot) Elder
Canada

Why is it taking so long? I want to have it finished already. I can't wait. I have other things to do.

No! Not me! I'm not ready. Let me finish these projects first, get my kids raised, and be *better.* Then I can do the work of the Creator.

It's strange, isn't it? The Creator just seems to have no sense of or respect for our concept of time!

❧

When you work for the Creator, you work in "his" time.

HUMILITY/BEING CALLED

We do not judge the mutants. We pray for them and release them as we pray and release ourselves. We pray they will look closely at their actions, at their values and learn before it is too late that all life is one. We pray they will stop the destruction of the earth and of each other.

> —Voice of the Aboriginal Elders
> As told to Marlo Morgan

In Marlo Morgan's story "Mutant Messenger," these words come from a group of Australian Aboriginals who, according to Morgan, have decided to leave the planet. They have made the choice not to reproduce and not to continue their race. They are leaving because their land and resources will no longer support them because of climatic changes and encroachment. They can see what is happening to the planet and they choose to leave.

In their leaving, there is no blame and no judgment. They ask us to look at what we are doing.

I hear this again and again from Native people—no blame, no judgment. They only ask us to *look* at what we're doing.

☯

We are being called to live another way. With loving prayers, we are being called.

❮◦❯❮◦❯❮◦❯❮◦❯❮◦❯❮◦❯❮◦❯❮◦❯❮◦❯❮◦❯❮◦❯❮◦❯❮◦❯❮◦❯❮◦❯

REALITY, OR SEEING IS NOT BELIEVING

Every eye forms its own fancy.

—*Mrs. O'Malley,* Irish Proverb

Each of us sees what we want to see. Because of this, we tend to ignore what we don't want to see. Also, we see what we have been trained to see, and we tend not to see anything that our worldview does not explain.

Hence, we build a world of constructs and concepts that may or may not have anything to do with reality. And if we think about reality, *whose* reality are we considering?

One of the problems with "white minds" is that we have come to believe that our reality is the *only* reality.

❧

There are many realities in this world. Do I have the ability to be open to those other than mine?

HELP FROM ANCESTORS

If what the *kahunas* [teachers] taught is true—that it is possible for an *aumatua* [an ancestral spirit for two generations like one's deceased parent or grandparent] to guard and inspire a beloved relative on earth—I shall watch over you from above and guide you righteously. I do not know at the present time how this is done but I shall find out from the *Hui O Aumatua* [guild of ancestral spirits] when I join them after I awaken from nature's trance-sleep of death.

—*Mary Julia Glennie Bush*
Hawaiian Kupuna

Christianity talks of guardian angels, yet cannot tolerate the idea of an *aumatua*. I like the idea that my mother, my grandmother, and my great-grandmother are guarding me and inspiring me.

This reminds me of a saying in the Twelve Step program of Alcoholics Anonymous: "You have to do it yourself. You do not have to do it alone."

I wonder what would happen if I allowed myself to use all the help that is available to me, seen and unseen?

☙

I know I need all the help I can get.

TOOLS FOR LIFE

This story is a lesson laying out a pattern for people to live by. People should live by choosing one another as friends, to be happy, to joke with one another, and to love one another.

—Peter Kalifornsky, Dena'ina Elder
Alaska

"To choose one another as friends." I have many friends throughout the world, and lately I have felt the need to nurture and support those friendships. For me, this means keeping in touch, arranging time to spend with my friends, and letting them know how important they are to me. Sometimes I feel there are too many of them for me to keep in contact with. But would I have them for friends if it were not important for me to be their friend?

"To be happy." Such a simple thing when we accept life on life's terms.

"To joke with one another." This is another easy one. In my family, teasing and joking were forms of intimacy. I find this to be true of most Native people as well.

"To love one another." First we must value ourselves. And what joy there is in loving one another!

◉

It's so simple. All we have to do is do it.

ADVERTISING

Chema chajiuza, kibaya chajitembeza.

A good thing sells itself. A bad thing is advertized.

—Swahili Proverb

I have observed this to be very true. In fact, I have noticed that there are many more ads for addictive agents—alcohol, drugs, tobacco, and sugar—than there are for things that are healthful. I have also noticed that children rarely see ads on television for healthful foods. The cereals "made for children" are usually full of sugar and have little nutritive value. I believe this is called "creating a market."

I recently talked with a woman who was "developing" a store on Fiji. I heard her say, "I put plastic wrap on the shelves. Can you believe it? They didn't even know they needed it until I started stocking it!" What's wrong with this picture?

⊙⊙

There is wisdom in attraction, not promotion.

WARRIORS

[Being a warrior] It is a willingness to sacrifice everything except your truth, your way of being, your commitment. The ultimate stand is to your commitment to do something with your life that will make a difference.

—*Douglas Cardinal*
Canadian Indian Architect, Writer, and Artist

Throughout the world, a new breed of warrior is being discussed. These warriors have nothing to do with weapons, battles, or killing. Rather, they are taking a stand on living. To fight for life and harmony as if each of our lives makes a difference is no small challenge.

To stand for our way of being in a closed system whose nature is to destroy everything unlike itself—and perhaps ultimately to destroy that closed system—is not easy. Instead, what if each of us is willing to do something with her or his life that would benefit at least seven generations to come? What if we become warriors for balance and healing?

Warriors don't always have to fight. They may just have to stand up.

VALUES

We Indians have a more human philosophy of life. We Indians will show this country how to act human. Someday this country will revise its Constitution, its laws, in terms of human beings instead of property. If Red Power is to be a power in this country it is because it is ideological. . . . . What is the ultimate value of a man's life? That is the question.

—*Vine Deloria, Jr.,* Sioux Writer
American Indian

Some years ago, I had the realization that no system built on economics alone had survived or would survive very long. In the Western world we have capitalism, communism, and socialism, and all are based upon economics.

What would a society look like that is based upon spiritual values instead of property? When we look at work, politics, natural resources, production, education, religion, and living in terms of spiritual values, we shift our perceptions, and hopefully our behavior.

ॐ

When I make my personal decisions in terms of my spiritual being instead of property, I have made a start.

ANGER

To hold on to one's anger for a long time is only to prolong one's unhappiness.

—*Asesela Ravuvu*, Fijian Writer

Fijian culture has long had ways of dealing with anger. They recognized that we only make *ourselves* unhappy by holding on to anger.

Anger is a human response to many situations. In some cultures, it is considered normal and is basically accepted. It is not a part of all Native cultures. However, in those cultures where expressing anger is an acceptable part of the culture, there are usually acceptable ways of dealing with it.

When we hold on to anger and do not deal with it, it becomes a cancer and infects not only the mind and feelings, but the soul and body as well.

Why prolong our unhappiness? For our own well-being, we need to learn ways of letting go of anger.

⟨o⟩⟨o⟩⟨o⟩⟨o⟩⟨o⟩⟨o⟩⟨o⟩⟨o⟩⟨o⟩⟨o⟩⟨o⟩⟨o⟩⟨o⟩⟨o⟩⟨o⟩⟨o⟩

ELDERS' TEACHINGS

Te Mana-O-Manutuke.

Youth talks–Age teaches.

—Maori Proverb

Often, those who have the least to say talk the most.

I have always respected my Elders as I was taught to do as a child. I was taught to listen to my Elders, and even though what they said sometimes did not seem particularly relevant to my life, I discovered that if I listened closely, I would always find what I needed.

As an adult, I am so grateful for these teachings. As I've been spending more and more time with Native Elders, I have learned that they do a lot of what sailors call tacking. When they want to get to the left, they go right, and when they want to go down, they go up or sideways. Only by staying with them and listening closely is it possible to put it all together. Life with the Elders is not linear, it moves in loops and spirals.

෧෧

The most important teachings are often the ones that require waiting with, and then the teaching may be learning to wait with.

SHARING IDEAS

It's not important that we get the idea across. It's important that we learn.

—*Alex Pua,* Hawaiian Elder

I used to be so attached to my ideas, and I even used to think they were mine! Somehow, it seemed possible to own ideas. I had given birth to them, and they were my babies. I owned them!

When I owned my ideas, I used to think that it was very important that others understood them and did so in the way I wanted them understood. I spent a lot of time explaining and convincing.

Then, I began to realize that I don't know where my ideas come from. They certainly aren't mine. They pop into my head from somewhere—and all I have to do is get out of the way. And now, since they are no longer "mine," I see that explaining and convincing are forms of control, and that when I do either, I am trying to control the perceptions of the listener. So now I just put them out and let them go. This approach to sharing ideas leaves much more time and energy for learning.

I am learning to share my ideas and let them go.

HONESTY

I always tell my grandson honest people is just like having money in the bank. Anybody can help you. Anybody can trust you. That's it. There's no other way around. That's how the Indians were.

—*Altona Brown,* Athabaskan Elder
Ruby, Alaska

Honesty is important as a way of life. What if our money in the bank is the experience people have of us and that we have of ourselves? There is a simple trust that exists in Native cultures. It is not that we need to be honest for other people. We need to be honest for ourselves. Not being honest does us more harm than it will ever do to anyone else. If you can trust yourself, then others can trust you.

Honesty as a cultural norm is even more important. I have often said that the addictive system in which we live is an illusory system. It is built on the illusion of control, the illusion of objectivity, and the illusion of perfection. I believe it is also immersed in confusion, dishonesty, and theoretical constructs that are built on abstractions and divorced from nature and reality.

Is it any wonder that honesty is not a cultural value in Western society?

OUR MOTHER EARTH

We grow up knowing that the land is our Mother. We know that
there can be no monetary value for our Mother.

—Maori Kaumātua (Elder)

For Maori people, the earth is not symbolically our Mother. The
earth *is* our Mother. We come from the earth and to the earth we
will return. The earth cares for us and gives us what we need for
shelter, food, and life. The earth grounds us and gives us our connection with all of life as well as our identity. The earth gives us our
place to stand. Our ancestors' bones return to the earth and feed the
earth, and out of their bones we grow our food.

If we sell our Mother, we get nothing in return. The money is
only symbolic and will last for the blink of an eye, while our
Mother is with us forever.

❧

How can we sell our Mother? How can we rape our Mother?

ILLNESS

Talking Health but Doing Sickness
          —Patricia Kinloch
          Health Services Researcher in Samoa

The quote above is the title of a book on Samoan health. I find it to be a very profound epigraph.

How often do we talk health and do sickness? We talk about ridding our people of disease and we support industries that release carcinogens into the air. We talk about healing, and we use drugs that have side effects that are later found to be lethal. We talk about raising healthy children and we isolate our young mothers with little or no support.

The Samoans see sickness as a disruption in the social order. Illness, in Samoan culture, is much bigger than germs and biology. They recognize that illness is not just an individual issue. It affects the community and the group to which the person belongs.

@@

It is important to see that even our ideas *about illness are culturally based.*

INHERITANCE

His race lives in him; he thinks as they thought, their loyalties are his; his memory goes back to their beginnings; their long experience is his counsellor.

—*Father Donnchadh O'Floinn*
Irish Priest

What is this inheritance? Do we have a genetic coding that goes far beyond physical characteristics? What do I carry in my memory that is a living link with my ancestors?

Sometimes I feel that my race lives in me. That I have a particular set of beliefs and values that belong not only to me but to my ancestors, who still think and feel within me, who are alive because of me and I am alive because of them.

I can see that my environment affects me, and yet it doesn't affect my inner being that much. Often, my inner being has beliefs and values that go far back, beyond anything I personally could have learned.

◎◎

If I have the long experience of my ancestors as my counselor, how can I use it most effectively?

◄◊►◄◊►◄◊►◄◊►◄◊►◄◊►◄◊►◄◊►◄◊►◄◊►◄◊►◄◊►◄◊►◄◊►◄◊►◄◊►◄◊►

DIVERSITY

The day Hawaiians disappear will be the day when the water no longer flows.

—Hawaiian Elder

I know when I heard this, my heart ached. I cannot imagine life without my Hawaiian friends. They add a dimension to my life that no one else does. I do not know exactly *what* that dimension is, and I know it is there.

We often hear about the whales disappearing or certain animals or cultures disappearing, and that this will mean the end of the world—as we know it.

What I have come to understand is that if we cannot save the redwoods or the whales or the Hawaiians, it is not their disappearance that is key. What is key is that we will have lost the level of consciousness that allows us to comprehend the importance of diversity to the survival of the planet. If we do not understand the need for diversity, nothing else matters.

❦

Nothing is as simple or as complex as it seems.

WAITING AND LISTENING

The bonds with the mythical Beings of the Dreamtime are such that they believe in a united world of body and spirit for every form of life in the land, both living and non-living. This then means that the rocks, rivers and waterholes are more than just a reminder or a symbol of the Dreamtime; they represent reality and eternal truth.

—*David Gulpilil,* Australian Aboriginal

From my time with Aboriginal Elders, I know that they share with me what I can handle and understand, and I also know that they are telling me more than I can understand at the present moment.

The Dreamtime is one experience where I know that without living with the Aboriginals for a long time, I will only have the most tentative grasp of what this Dreamtime really is.

I understand that, like all Native people, the Australian Aboriginal knows the oneness of all things. Even when I get just the slightest notion of "a united world of body and spirit for every form of life in the land, both living and non-living"—my universe expands.

Even when I can't *know* because of my cultural limitations, I can *sense* that there is something here that is important for me to open up to.

❀

If the land represents reality and eternal truth, what does that mean for me and the way I live?

SILENT NATURE

If you want to get the fish back, you have to stop. In September, the *'oama* [fish] come. We used to throw net right out there and catch plenty, but no more. We used to throw net and catch crab. Every time you throw, you get two or three. No more. We used to have *hukilau* [fishing] right here.

—*Kaipo Chandler,* Hawaiian Kupuna

Kaipo Chandler has not accepted the inevitable, that nature will disappear. And when the fish disappear, he knows that something is wrong.

As I write this, I am looking out over the lovely countryside of Tuscany, Italy. The mountains and hills and trees are beautiful. I just heard a songbird, and my heart leaped. There are so very few songbirds here. There is an unearthly silence. Italy is one of the few countries where hunters are permitted to kill songbirds for sport. This is such a rich land, economically, that there is no need for the birds as food. We do see, however, nattily attired hunters with proper hunting boots and vests, carrying shotguns and leading dogs to kill the few birds that are left. The only nature sounds are those of insects—and they thrive!

The lovely songs of the birds make them easy targets. This silence hits me as the silence of the death of nature.

❧

How grateful I am for the songbirds! How empty our world without them.

◄O►◄O►◄O►◄O►◄O►◄O►◄O►◄O►◄O►◄O►◄O►◄O►◄O►◄O►◄O►◄O►

LIFE/DEATH—TRANSITIONS

What is life? It is the flash of a firefly in the night. It is the breath of a buffalo in the winter time. It is the little shadow which runs across the grass and loses itself in the Sunset.

—*Crowfoot,* Blackfoot Elder
Bow River, Canada

These words about life were spoken in the dying hours of Crowfoot. Not only is he a great speaker and poet, but in his dying words he gives us one of the great gifts of the Indian. He gives the knowledge and the comfort of the living circle of life.

Death is not an ending. It is only one phase in the never-ending circle of life as we go from childhood to adolescence to adulthood to the second childhood of old age. Life is not linear—stopping and starting. Death is but a transition to the next phase in the circle. As we come to know and live the circle, we feel no fear, no anxiety. There are only transitions that affirm the living.

๑๑

The circle, the Medicine Wheel, is a gift of life.

UNSEEN/UNKNOWN

And from no point better than Tara, which was once the magical and political centre of the Sacred Island, could we begin our study of the Irish Fairy-Faith. Though the Hill has lain un-ploughed and deserted since the curses of Christian priests fell upon it, on the calm air of summer evenings, at the twilight hour, wondrous music still sounds over its slopes, and at night long, weird processions of silent spirits march round its grass-grown *raths* and *forts*. It is only men who fear the curse of the Christians; the fairy-folk regard it not.

—*W. Y. Evans-Wentz,* Writer on Irish Lore

How much is out there in the mystery of life that I know noth-ing about? How much do I know nothing about because my mind has been trained to be closed to phenomena that I cannot perceive and understand with my senses and technology and that cannot be explained by modern science?

Why does the Church come up again and again as the prime de-fender of the faith of modern science? What is the relationship be-tween the witch-hunts against healers of the Middle Ages, the wiping out of Native healers in colonized countries, and the witch-hunts that are occurring in the helping professions today? What did my ancestors know that I have not had the opportunity to learn—and even to reject, if I want?

෨෩

Lots of questions. Not very many answers.

SCIENCE AND TECHNOLOGY

Centuries ago you white people chose the path of science and technology. That path will destroy the planet. Our role is to protect the planet. We are hoping that you discover this before it's too late.

> —*Reuben Kelly,* Elder
> Thainghetti People, Gurrigan Clan
> Koorie [Australian Aboriginal]

"You white people." I hear that a lot. What's most important in what Mr. Kelly said was that centuries ago, we chose a path of science and technology. It has taken me years of study to see the role that Western science and technology have had in the present state of the world. Mr. Kelly knew these issues all along from his myths and legends. Would we have been better off if we had started listening to him and his people some time ago?

We have a big transition ahead of us. It is not just technology that's the problem. It is the worldview that results in technology. If we changed our worldview, and consequently the values and decisions that come out of that worldview—we would, by default, change the technology we devise and what we do with it.

But worldviews aren't changed overnight. If we set up something that seems impossible, we'll just give up and not even start.

꩜

I only can move as my process unfolds. What I can do is pray for openness and willingness and seek information and awareness.

OPENNESS

It's happening all over the country and the same thing is coming about a new life, a new reconnection, and a new relationship, trying to understand what the Creator meant for us to do.
—*George Goodstriker*, Kainai (Blackfoot) Elder
Canada

Something is happening all over the country—and all over the world. Voices are speaking up that have long held their silence. Ideas and ceremonies that were believed to have been destroyed are emerging from their hiding places in the minds and hearts of Native people. There is ferment and a growth of a new energy and a commitment to bring important knowledge.

In return, we have an opportunity not to be threatened or arrogant. We have the opportunity to open our beings to teachings that can soothe our souls and heal our planet. The choice is ours.

❦

Together, we can "understand what the Creator meant for us to do."

UNSEEN POWERS

I know that our people possessed remarkable powers of concentration and abstraction, and I sometimes fancy that such nearness to nature as I have described keeps the spirit sensitive to impressions not commonly felt, and in touch with the unseen powers.
—*Ohiyesa (Charles Eastman)*, Santee Dakota Writer
American Indian

My mother was such a person. She grew up among the Cherokee and was adopted by them. She always maintained a nearness to nature, and regardless of where we lived, she insisted that we go back every year to the place of her roots to reconnect with the land. She is buried there, at the end of the Cherokee "Trail of Tears."

I am so glad that she maintained her nearness to nature that kept her spirit "sensitive to impressions not commonly felt." She suffered a great deal for her relationship with the unseen powers. Although her relationship with the world of nature was keenly felt by her, she had little support for this gift either from my stepfather, who was an engineer, or from white culture in general, which gave her the message that she might be crazy because she was in touch with "unseen powers."

I am glad for who my mother was and I am grateful for what she taught me.

We come into our own when we can see the gifts our parents have been for us.

◄◊► ◄◊► ◄◊► ◄◊► ◄◊► ◄◊► ◄◊► ◄◊► ◄◊► ◄◊► ◄◊► ◄◊► ◄◊► ◄◊► ◄◊► ◄◊►

FORCES UNKNOWN

Do not take lava rock away from Hawai'i. It will bring you bad luck.

—Hawaiian Folk Wisdom

I have heard my Hawaiian friends say that rocks should never be removed from a *heiau* [temple], and that big lava rocks should never be removed from a stream.

Tourists are frequently warned about not carrying rocks off from Hawaii and they do it anyway. The funny thing is that the Hawaiian tourist bureau and the local post offices keep getting rocks mailed back to them.

Tourists do not heed the warning—and they have bad luck! It seems to stop when they mail the rocks back. It's not scientific . . . it's just experience.

☯

Don't take rocks from Hawaii!

COMMUNITY AND SURVIVAL

It was impossible to live in one place and survive.
—*Al Wright*, Athabaskan-Anglo Elder
Minto, Alaska

One of the things I hear again and again from Native people about being colonized by Western culture is that Native people are forced to settle in little houses on single plots of ground with their immediate families.

This is a very effective way of destroying their lifestyle, of controlling their food supply, and of controlling them. And it is more than that. It is a way of destroying their community.

Why is it that Western culture pushes the nuclear family as the basic building block of society, when all ancient cultures see extended families and the whole community as the basic unit of society? What kind of people are we producing in Western culture when we force them to live in isolated units that cannot possibly meet their needs?

Why is it that right now Western governments are increasingly pushing the isolated nuclear family as society's building block?

@&

We need community support to grow and thrive. What would our world look like if our building blocks were communities?

THE CHILDREN

Take care of our children
Take care of what they hear
Take care of what they see
Take care of what they feel.

For how the children grow so will be the shape of Aotearoa.
—*Dame Whina Cooper,* Maori Kuia (Elder)

This prayer was given to me by Dame Whina as we shared time together. I felt honored to be with her. While she still creates controversy at age ninety-six, no one disagrees with what she has to say about caring for our children.

It is the height of civilized behavior to care for our children and our old people. It is a door to our spirituality to care for all children and Elders.

It seems so trite to say that children are our future, and I wonder how many of us act as if we truly believe this. What kind of world would we fashion if we truly took care of what our children hear, see, and feel?

We can know the future only in the laughter of healthy children.

◄◌►◄◌►◄◌►◄◌►◄◌►◄◌►◄◌►◄◌►◄◌►◄◌►◄◌►◄◌►◄◌►◄◌►◄◌►

LIFE/DEATH

The Ladakhi conception of reality is circular, one of a constant returning. There is not the sense that this life is the only opportunity. Death is as much a beginning as an end, a passing from one birth to the next, not a final dissolution.

—*Helena Norberg-Hodge*
On the Ladakh of Tibet

So many Native people talk about life as a never-ending circle in which we move. There is something comforting about a circle. There is freedom in a circle because we know that we will be returning. We find circles in nature often.

We talk about death as being a new beginning—as entering a new life—and yet we don't act as if we believe it.

What if I really believed my life is a circle among many circles and I have only to participate and not worry about the circle suddenly becoming linear?

🌀

How would I live if I truly believed that I will infinitely move in the circle of life?

OCTOBER

◄◇►◄◇►◄◇►◄◇►◄◇►◄◇►◄◇►◄◇►◄◇►◄◇►◄◇►◄◇►◄◇►◄◇►◄◇►

EQUALITY

In the Maori system one expects to approach the key decision maker on an equal basis with "eyeball to eyeball" communication. In other words the individual that is being approached cannot hide behind a system.

—*Rangimarie Turuki Pere*, Maori Writer

When we live within a hierarchy, people are always hiding behind the system or their roles.

The Maori can help us learn that as human beings, we are all equal. We are all made by the Creator, and the Creator does not assign status or hierarchy.

I am responsible for my feeling of equality. If I go "one-down," I am the one who does it. If I go "one-up," I am the one who does it. *And* it helps to have a system where people are believed to be equal because they are.

๑๑

When I hide behind a system or let others do it, I am contributing to inequality.

◄○►◄○►◄○►◄○►◄○►◄○►◄○►◄○►◄○►◄○►◄○►◄○►◄○►◄○►◄○►◄○►◄○►

THE ABSENCE OF THE SACRED

In the absence of the sacred—nothing is sacred—everything is for sale.

> —*Oren Lyons,* Onondaga Tribal Chief
> American Indian

What does it mean to live life in the "absence of the sacred"?

I was recently in New Zealand talking with a master carver of the ancient Maori tradition. He told me about old carved pieces that had powerful *mana* (power) and were treated with great care and attention because they were sacred. I tried to think what in our culture would be handled with the same reverence and care, and I couldn't think of anything.

Have we become a culture with an "absence of the sacred"? We have religious relics and temples, but do we have the sacred? In Western culture, almost everything is for sale, and it's assumed that "everything has its price." This has become such a fact of life that romantic stories have been written about how unusual it is when someone is not willing to sell at any price.

◎

In the absence of the sacred—everything is for sale and life has no value.

OWNERSHIP

Europeans and their perception of land is based on the materialistic. They look upon land as "my land, I own that land." It is a commodity. Whereas Aboriginals look at something as a part of the whole, a part of themselves, and they are part of that—the land. The land and they are one.

> —One of seven Aboriginals speaking about Musgrave Park Australia

We not only treat the land as a commodity, we treat ourselves and much of our lives as commodities. For example, the copyright laws put us in a position of treating our words and our books as commodities because we think we own them. What a put-down of our productions when we make them commodities instead of creations. When we realize that we are part of a whole and that who we are and what we have are part of a whole and a gift of the Creator, it makes ownership seem a little silly.

◎◎

If I am one with all Creation, I participate in sharing.

◄◦►◄◦►◄◦►◄◦►◄◦►◄◦►◄◦►◄◦►◄◦►◄◦►◄◦►◄◦►◄◦►◄◦►◄◦►◄◦►

REALITIES

The woman was considered the equal if not *the* most important because she was the basis of the family.

—*Alex Pua,* Hawaiian Elder

In cultures where the family, the community, and the future generations are valued, women are valued.

Women's liberation may mean not being as active as the male culture has been in destroying the world. Equality for women may well mean having our particular, peculiar perspective honored and inviting that perspective to influence what we do in this world.

I know that as a woman, my woman's reality is very close to Native reality. Neither of us is crazy. Our reality needs to be heard and respected.

❦

Women are not only responsible for bringing future generations into the world, we are responsible for joining with others who want to make certain that we have a future.

FEELINGS

In the province of Munster it is a common thing for the women to follow a funeral, to join in the universal cry with all their might and main for some time, and then to turn and ask—"Arragh! who is it that's dead? Who is it that we are crying for?"

—*Moira Edgeworth* (1767–1849)
Irish

What a delight! If grieving is what you do well, why not do it at every opportunity?

If there is one thing the Irish know how to do, it is how to express their feelings. At least that was the belief in our Irish household.

Anger was quick, expressed, to the point, and forgotten. There was no need to linger with it. Tears flowed easily for ourselves and others and often out of pure joy. Sadness and grieving were accepted and felt as a part of life.

෨෨

Feelings just are. To express them is a skill and a gift.

COMMITMENTS

We know we're going to get paid no matter what. Even if they went broke, they'd work the rest of their life to pay us off because that's the kind of people they are. That's why we like to deal with them. If they say something, that's the way it is.
—*Al Wright,* Athabaskan–Anglo Elder
Minto, Alaska

It's good to be able to trust people. To know that they take responsibility for their promises and their commitments.

I believe that one of the qualities of adulthood is willingness to deal with the consequences of one's decisions and commitments. If we close a deal or make an agreement that we later want to renegotiate, and the other person doesn't want to, it is our responsibility to follow through on our commitment. We can just consider it the tuition that we're paying for the learning.

☙❧

Not following through on an agreement or commitment is much more costly—to our souls—than doing it, even if we don't like it.

DISHONESTY

When you lie to a person, you hurt his soul.
—*Phil Lane, Sr.,* Yankton Lakota Elder
American Indian

When we lie, we put two souls in jeopardy. Probably our own is the most damaged when we lie, but there is nothing more destructive to relationships than lying. Even when we think we're getting away with a lie, we know it, and if those to whom we lie are in touch with themselves at all, they "feel" our dishonesty. Lying is one of the most expensive things we do in life, and there are no long-range rewards.

When we make truth-speaking a way of life, we need only tell the truth about ourselves. Then others have to take responsibility for their own truth-speaking.

&

When I speak the truth as best I can, I am adding to the healing energy of the planet.

VICTIM/PERPETRATOR

Europeans caught a glimpse of Aboriginal personality. Governor Phillip had decided to set an example by punishing a convict thief who stole some fishing implements belonging to an Aboriginal person. In the presence of both the British and Aboriginal People the thief was bound and flogged. So distressed were the Aboriginals that they attacked the flogger, took the whip from him and cried for the thief.

—*Burnum Burnum*
Australian Aboriginal Writer

I love this story. When I first read it, I paused and looked inside to discover with amazement just how deep was my training in punishment and victim/perpetrator. Of course the man should be punished if he stole something, especially if he took it from some gentle Australian Aboriginal! Then I stopped. What have I to learn from this story?

Not too long ago, I was sued. When I was served the papers, I was incredulous. How could this happen? There must be some misunderstanding. Everyone knows what the truth is. My next thought—coming very quickly—was, "I'll not only prove my innocence, I'll *get* her." Then I stopped, shocked, and I prayed. It was clear to me that my issue for this process was to not take on the victim/perpetrator dualism. Every perpetrator has been a victim, and every person who believes she is a victim will become a perpetrator. Regardless of the outcome, my spiritual issue was not to take on this dualism.

@@

I have a lot to learn from looking at my victim/perpetrator training and from refusing to participate in this way of thinking.

DREAMING REALITY

Aboriginal peoples live in the dream state of vision. As Native people we are trained to bring dreams up into reality, into the real world. As a Native person I am trained to bring out people's visions. I am a dream maker trained to make people's dreams a reality. I am totally involved in a dream in the making.

—Douglas Cardinal
Canadian Indian Architect, Writer, and Artist

To live in the dream state of vision is to live in a state of oneness with the Creator and to participate in the movement toward a future of becoming who we can be as a person and as a race.

We can be trained to be engineers, physicians, ministers, teachers, even psychologists, but what do we know about bringing out people's visions?

How can we trust our dreams to join the flow of all humanity and to participate in the flow of the Creator?

☙❧

If Native people are "trained to bring dreams up into reality," we can open ourselves to learn from them.

INFORMATION/WISDOM

Just because I don't have a degree, I don't know anything. . . .
They [college graduates who work for Fish and Game] tell me all
about what's going on with animals and they think they've got it
wired, but they don't know one lousy thing except what they
read out of a book. And half the stuff they read in a book is
wrong because the guy who wrote it didn't know nothing about
it. But it's gospel once it's in writing.

—*Al Wright,* Athabaskan-Anglo Elder
Minto, Alaska

He doesn't mince words. Native people have generations of
wisdom about fish and game at their disposal. The problem is that
this information does not easily fit into a mechanistic scientific
worldview.

Why is it that we have to try to make someone else feel ignorant
when we don't know what they know and they don't know what
we know?

@@

There's lots of information in books. There's lots of wisdom in people. Both are necessary.

◄O►◄O►◄O►◄O►◄O►◄O►◄O►◄O►◄O►◄O►◄O►◄O►◄O►◄O►◄O►◄O►◄O►

UNFAIRNESS

Unfairness occurs when one group is dealt with in terms of another group's culture.

—*Hiwi Tauroa*, Maori Writer

This is an important statement to ponder. It is difficult for us to divorce ourselves from our system and our worldview. Any of us would struggle with that.

However, it is important for us to get enough information to see that our perception of reality and what we consider to be right and wrong is determined by our worldview. We all have the ability to learn that our particular worldview is not necessarily the "right" or the only worldview. After we realize that, it's time to watch and listen.

To be respectful of another's culture and not to deal with it in terms of our own is a great skill, indeed.

❧

Perhaps, if I really try, I will not contribute to the total mass of unfairness in the world.

❖─❖─❖─❖─❖─❖─❖─❖─❖─❖─❖─❖─❖─❖─❖─❖─❖─❖─❖

BELONGING

We've got our culture, we've still got our old ways of living. We might live in a white man's home but we still have our black way, an Aboriginal way, because we live our life. My tribe is Morowori, my father tribe, and I take after my father, because my father's name is Muri Goodgebah and that means a flower or a tree. This is my land. We own this land, us Aboriginals. We were first here, before Captain Cook came. This is my land, here, where I look. We own all this, every little bush, every little tree, every log, every stick, every little bit of flower. You see those big flowers? Emus are getting fat now and they're ready to lay. We tell by the flowers because they're getting near springtime. This is our land. This is not your land.

> —Five Aboriginals talking about life in Brewarrina Australia

When I read the above, I was filled with such a gentle, steadfast, quiet feeling of belonging. This person belongs. He knows who he is, and he knows his ancestors and his tribe. He knows his land and he knows every bush and tree on that land. He knows the voice of the land and the way it speaks.

It takes time to know these things—perhaps thousands of years.

❧

When I know where I belong, I know myself.

⊸⟨0⟩⊷⟨0⟩⊷⟨0⟩⊷⟨0⟩⊷⟨0⟩⊷⟨0⟩⊷⟨0⟩⊷⟨0⟩⊷⟨0⟩⊷⟨0⟩⊷⟨0⟩⊷⟨0⟩⊷⟨0⟩⊷⟨0⟩⊷

HEALTH

No time for your health today; no health for your time tomorrow.
—Irish Proverb

We treat our bodies like machines. We believe we can fix them and get new parts. Our children learn to respect their bodies only when they don't work right.

Now is the time to begin doing what we were going to start tomorrow. Good health is not something we can buy. However, it can be an extremely valuable savings account.

Health, especially in an unhealthy society, takes time, energy, and commitment.

We can influence who we will be tomorrow, for tomorrow can only be built on today.

@๑

Looking after my health today gives me a better hope for tomorrow.

DIFFERENCES

The culture that primarily values technology or individualism is definitely objective, while a culture that values the family, nature, and the celebration of life is surely identified as subjective. Whether you are Hawaiian or not, if you primarily relate to life and people on a personal level, you are subjective and have a major conflict of interest in the present Western objective style of ethics.

—*Patrick Ka'ano'i,* Hawaiian Writer

I felt such relief when I read the above passage! Naming is always such a great gift.

As I have spent time with Native people, I have realized that I feel more at home with them. In addition, I have had a progressive feeling as I come back into Western culture that the battering I sometimes feel must be a very small taste of what it must have been like and how it still is for Native people the world over, trying to cope with and share their wisdom with Western minds.

∞

Where differences are respected, there is no need to batter.

GENTLENESS

"If you're going to break the branches off, talk to it. They're your friends." Grandma told them what to do. Exactly what to do and how to do it. "Don't rush. That's your friend," she said. "If you're gonna break it off or chop on it, you talk to it before you hurt it. They used to be people. Those trees used to be people long, long time ago. And they became a tree. Good people. That's why they live today. Still here."

—*Altona Brown*, Athabaskan Elder
Ruby, Alaska

What a gift to live gently with the world around us! We ask permission before we take something from our friends—or at least we should.

We interact with friends in a way that is good for us and good for them—or at least we should.

We move with respect toward those that shelter and care for us—or at least we should.

@@

When I remember that trees are my friends who give me fresh oxygen to breathe, shade, shelter, and protection, I am reminded to be respectful.

TAKE TIME

Measure twice and cut once.

—*Peter Davitt*, Irish Proverb

Peter mumbled this proverb to us as we were doing something over again that we had not measured carefully in the first place. I liked the proverb and I remembered it. I often mumble it to myself.

How important, and efficient, it is to take the time to do things consciously! When I'm rushing, I'm almost always not paying attention. And when I am not paying attention to what I'm doing, accidents happen or I make mistakes. I can learn from my mistakes, and what I usually learn is not to rush.

When I take time with my life, I have more opportunity to live it.

◄O►◄O►◄O►◄O►◄O►◄O►◄O►◄O►◄O►◄O►◄O►◄O►◄O►◄O►◄O►◄O►◄O►

COMMUNITY

All affirmed the central role of Indian prophecy, the bond between Indians and "Mother Earth," the existence of sacred
"powers" by which ritual specialists benefitted their people. They
agreed to restore spiritual practices, encourage native language
use, and combat alcoholism and family disintegration.
> —*Little Star,* Tribe Unknown
> American Indian

Native people are on the move. As a community, they are trying
to reestablish their spirituality and reaffirm their care for and respect
for and valuing of "Mother Earth." This return to the "old ways" is
supported by their speaking their own original spiritual, nonmecha-
nistic languages and by their participation in ritual and ceremony.

Throughout the world, I see Native cultures moving to reconnect on a community level. Alcoholism and family disintegration
can only be healed at a systemic, community level.

ஒ

No family can heal without community.

CENSORSHIP

Ulimi wangu umetiwa kulabu hauwezi kunena.

My tongue has had a hook put in it, it cannot speak (censored).
—Swahili Proverb

Often, as I share my perceptions of a particular situation, I am told I'm so brave and so courageous. I am often startled by this response, and wonder how and why we are taught not to speak our truth.

Someone once gave me a Russian poem—the exact poem and the name of the poet long lost and forgotten. The poem questioned what kind of world we have created where the simple speaking of the truth as we see it is seen as courageous.

I believe it is important to see if we censor our own truth-speaking or if truth-speaking is censored by our society, or both.

☯

A culture (or a person) that cannot stand the truth cannot stand itself.

LEVELS OF TRUTH

Hawaiians speak on three different levels. There's the mundane (physical), the symbolic, and then there's the spiritual level. There are meanings on all these levels. That's the way it is with the body too. Feeling happens on a cellular level. While we are loving the body, we are healing on a cellular level.

—*Angeline Locey*
Hawaiian Healer and Kupuna

I have heard again and again from Hawaiians that "missionary Hawaiian" is a mechanical language but that the real Hawaiian language operates on several levels at the same time. The Hawaiians are acutely aware of the physical, the symbolic, and the spiritual.

When we heal, all of these levels interact. Hawaiian healers know that we have to heal on all levels or the physical body will not respond.

☯

When we respect our levels of truth, the truth heals on many levels.

WRONGING OURSELVES

Do no wrong nor hate your neighbor; for it is not he that you wrong; you wrong yourself.

—Shawnee Chant
American Indian

How little time we take to look at the way we wrong ourselves! Whenever I hate or do something destructive to someone else, it is truly myself I destroy.

Hatred is like cancer. It eats away at our souls and gnaws away at our inner beings. How important it is to let go of our resentments and make ourselves right with those whom we have wronged.

Yet, how often we leave out the next step of forgiving ourselves and making everything right with ourselves.

Amends to others are very important. Amends to ourselves are essential!

◄O►◄O►◄O►◄O►◄O►◄O►◄O►◄O►◄O►◄O►◄O►◄O►◄O►◄O►◄O►◄O►◄O►

AROHA

Aroha, expressed properly, imposed a commitment of a relationship with all people with whom one had contact. It was not possible to show *aroha* for one group of people whom one liked, and be free to express dislike or hatred of another group.

Aroha was a commitment. It was a challenging commitment. To express it to its fullest, required courage. It would require hard work to develop this particular kind of relationship and to express it to all people at all times. A commitment to show *aroha* was exciting, but very, very exhausting.

—*Hiwi Tauroa,* Maori Writer

Aroha is more than loving one's neighbor. It is more than loving one's enemies. It is loving all people equally. I have experienced this *aroha* of the Maori, and sometimes I need to be reminded of it.

It is so easy to be loving toward the people I know and like. It is even easy, most times, genuinely to feel loving toward my enemies because they are few and I can see that they face the same struggles as I do.

And to live *aroha*, which is the cornerstone of Maori culture, one must have the courage to develop relationships filled with *aroha* and to express it to all people at all times.

@@

Aroha *is not possible unless we truly know in our heart of hearts that we are all interconnected—that we are one.*

REALITY

Mpiima teseera: omwoyo gwe guseera.

It is not the knife that is cheating: but the spirit is cheating.
—Ugandan Proverb

For example, when the portion of meat cut is not what it is said to be, it is not the fault of the knife but the spirit of the person cutting that is cheating.

This proverb always makes me stop and think. Sometimes it is difficult for us to see the truth about a person. There is a big part of me that wants people to be the way I want them to be and I refuse to see the truth about them.

I was trained to believe that good Christians see the best in people, but in our dualistic society that means refusing to see the bad. It is always easier to blame something else (the knife, parents, society) for what people do, especially those who are close to us.

Slowly, I learned that it is disrespectful not to see people as they are. It is disrespectful to project onto them what we want them to be.

❀

When I accept what the spirit is doing, I can better deal with my reality.

POWER

When you're doing a good job, you can feel the *mana* of the wall.
—Hawaiian Elder

When building a wall, it is important just to build the wall.

What a great feeling it is to do whatever work we are doing with a focus that lets us feel the *mana* [power] of what we are doing.

In God's eyes, there is no small or large task, there is no significant or insignificant task. There is just the task at hand. When we focus on the task at hand, we and that task become one, sharing and augmenting the power that each of us brings to it, supported and loved into being by the Creator of us all.

When I am one with the Creator, the jobs I do are good jobs full of mana.

◄○►◄○►◄○►◄○►◄○►◄○►◄○►◄○►◄○►◄○►◄○►◄○►◄○►◄○►◄○►◄○►◄○►◄○►

SILENCE

Silence was meaningful with the Lakota, and his granting a space of silence before talking was done in the practice of true politeness and regardful of the rule that "thought comes before speech."

—*Chief Luther Standing Bear,* Oglala (Teton) Sioux Elder American Indian

When I read this, I tried to imagine a corporate board meeting that starts with silence. I remembered once consulting with a corporate committee faced with making a rather difficult decision. It was discussed at length, and as I was observing the discussion, I was aware that there was a lot of confusion. I saw several people trying to "be fair." I saw others trying to protect what they *thought* others wanted. I saw some stubbornly digging into their position. And so it went.

Then I asked everyone just to be quiet, go inside, and see if they could *discover* the decision that they already knew. We sat in silence for several minutes. I then went around the group and asked each person to state what she or he knew the decision to be. We had total consensus!

◎◎

Silence before talking can save a lot of time and energy.

WISDOM

Nor can traditional Native American life be called "simple" or "primitive" in an intellectual sense. A typical Elder of the Wauja people in the Amoxan rain forest, for example, has memorized hundreds of sacred songs and stories; plays several musical instruments; and knows the habits and habitats of hundreds of forest animals, birds and insects, as well as the medicinal uses of local plants. He can guide his sons in building a two story tall house using only axes, machetes and materials from the forest. He is an expert agronomist. He speaks several languages fluently; knows precisely how he is related to several hundred of his closest kin; and has acquired sufficient wisdom to share his home peacefully with in-laws, cousins, children and grandchildren. Female Elders are comparably learned and accomplished.

—*Philip Tojitsu Nash* and *Emilienne Ireland*
Writing about the Wauja of Guatemala

How impressive to see what people *can* do when they cease to focus upon what they cannot do! How impressive when we imagine the vast number of skills amassed by all the beings on this earth that are available to us if we are willing to accept our differences and listen! Wisdom comes in all colors, sizes, shapes, languages, and cultural forms.

I am the one who imposes limits—not the world around me.

◄O►◄O►◄O►◄O►◄O►◄O►◄O►◄O►◄O►◄O►◄O►◄O►◄O►◄O►◄O►◄O►

THE SERENADE OF NATURE

Listen to the serenade of nature singing the Song of God. The voice that floats on the wings of the wind, to those who are able to hear, is Love's celestial Song of Love that will drive away all fears.

—Old Native Hawaiian Fisherwoman

Nature is in continuous melody. The stream that flows has a million voices that calm, challenge, and move us with a rhythm that augments our own.

The wind in all its forms reminds us that we are not alone in this world, and whether it caresses the sweat from our bodies, or levels us with its enormous power, we hear the voice of God.

The earth itself responds to our listening and sends us the whispers that only the practiced ear can record.

☯

Only when we are one with all of nature will fear change to serenity.

◄०►◄०►◄०►◄०►◄०►◄०►◄०►◄०►◄०►◄०►◄०►◄०►◄०►◄०►◄०►◄०►◄०►

THE EARTH

I will help—with their schoolwork—Dad and Mum couldn't help us because they know little of such things—their knowledge was of the earth and loving the earth and that seemed more important.

—*Witi Ihimaera*, Maori Writer

"Their knowledge was of the earth and loving the earth and that seemed more important."

How lucky we are if we have teachers in our life who can teach us about the earth and loving the earth and all Creation! I have had many such teachers in my life: my mother, Elders, friends, and tribal teachers. All have shared just a little of their wisdom about loving the earth and their knowledge and understanding about it.

I see my grandson's fascination with bugs and the crawling things whose homes are in the earth, and now I, too, have the opportunity to pass on this knowledge and loving that have been so tenderly shared with me.

೦ಾ

To know and love the earth is to have roots and be a part of the cycle of life.

HUMILITY

These helpers are the entire 405 good spirits who serve *Wakan-Tanka* and Grandfather. These helper spirits belong to him, and if *Wakan-Tanka*, God, should take them from me, I will be just an ordinary man again. The good spirits are the ones who perform the great things through my mind and body. So while it is hard to serve God, it is at the same time an honor and rewarding to be his instrument in healing sick people and helping others to solve their problems.

—*Frank Fools Crow*, Ceremonial Chief and Medicine Man
Lakota Sioux
American Indian

Frank Fools Crow had great powers to heal, see the future, and travel out of his body, and he was a humble man of simplicity and love. He never took Wakan-Tanka for granted and many times a day expressed his gratitude in prayer and ceremony. In being around him, there was never any doubt that one was in the presence of a very holy man.

So often, we think that if we can just get the secrets and the ceremonies of such a person, we will have his power. Not so! Frank Fools Crow's power was in his humility and in his constant willingness to serve Wakan-Tanka in whatever way was needed.

@

Humility is a gift of prayer, ceremony, and willingness to serve. We can't make it happen.

◄◇►◄◇►◄◇►◄◇►◄◇►◄◇►◄◇►◄◇►◄◇►◄◇►◄◇►◄◇►◄◇►◄◇►◄◇►◄◇►◄◇►

ILLNESS

Despite the fact that Samoan people see sickness as inevitable, they also seek cares and cures. For them physical symptoms, a sick body, is not a sign of a "mechanical failure" but of the potential, and frequently real, sickness of the spirit. Spirit sickness is immanent in all Samoan sickness events.
—*Patricia Kinloch*
Health Services Researcher in Samoa

In her fascinating booklet, the writer suggests that Westerners tend, from our mechanistic science, to look at illness as some sort of biological, mechanical failure. We believe that if the failure is just diagnosed correctly and fixed, or if a new part can be found, we can and *should* be as good as new. There is little recognition that most illness involves a sickness of the spirit. Even an illness such as cancer after exposure to carcinogens may be a sickness of the spirit of a society that is more focused on money than clean air, fresh water, and healthy food.

Illness is very complex, and there are many perspectives from which to understand it. The Samoans have something to teach us about health and illness, if we are ready to learn.

☯

I am more than a machine.

◄◦►◄◦►◄◦►◄◦►◄◦►◄◦►◄◦►◄◦►◄◦►◄◦►◄◦►◄◦►◄◦►◄◦►◄◦►◄◦►

MOVING TOWARD WHOLENESS

The welfare of the people was what was important. In ceremonies held early in their lives, children were taught to think of
what was best for the tribe as a whole. Being selfish or thinking
only of oneself was unheard of.

—Aboriginal Wisdom

In Western culture, we seem to have set up a dualism: I do what is
good for the community/I have to deny myself.

Native people do not operate out of that dualism. Native children from very early on are taught to think beyond themselves, to
see themselves as an integral part of an ever-expanding whole in
which they are active participants. Their worldview moves them
from the individual to the community to the whole.

Our Western reductionist scientific worldview moves us into
smaller and smaller circles of self-centeredness.

෧෧

*Can it be that what is best for the community, for the whole, is in-
deed what is best for me?*

◄◊►◄◊►◄◊►◄◊►◄◊►◄◊►◄◊►◄◊►◄◊►◄◊►◄◊►◄◊►◄◊►◄◊►◄◊►

BEAUTY—ACCEPTANCE

And even if this trial should detect a flaw, this flaw most often is known only to its creator. So you see, the flaw should not take away from the overall form, beauty and essence of the vessel. . . . In the same way, a flaw in your own life, which *often* cannot be seen by others, should not keep you from reflecting your overall form and beauty.

> —*Al Qöyawayma,* Hopi Potter, Sculptor, and Engineer
> American Indian

How simple! Our flaws need not keep us from reflecting our "overall form and beauty."

When we see ourselves as a whole, all the pieces come together to form something more than what may be inherent in the separate pieces. Each of us as a being is a whole and therefore each of us is a being of beauty.

Our Creator knows our flaws and still we are accepted, just as this Hopi artist accepts his magnificent pots. What right have we to focus upon our flaws and miss the whole?

◎◎

My overall form and beauty transcend my flaws. My task is to accept life on life's terms and just to live it.

NOVEMBER

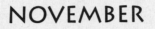

CONSERVATION

The Indian was a natural conservationist. He destroyed nothing, great or small. Destruction was not a part of Indian thought and action; if it had been, and had the man been the ruthless savage he has been accredited with being, he would have long ago preceded the European in the labor of destroying the natural life of this continent. The Indian was frugal in the midst of plenty. When the buffalo roamed the plains in multitudes he slaughtered only what he could eat and these he used to the hair and bones.

I know of no species of plant, bird or animal that were exterminated until the coming of the white man.

—*Chief Luther Standing Bear,* Oglala (Teton) Sioux American Indian

Many people are aware that we have environmental problems so serious that they constitute a global crisis. Yet, we have on this planet groups of people who have lived comfortably with the earth for thousands of years. In Western culture, we believe that science and technology will have the answers to our environmental crisis, while, at the same time, we refuse to see that our use of science and technology is creating these problems. We cannot continue to use science and technology to create a "better" world unless we change the worldview, beliefs, and value system with which we approach the planet. A quick technological "fix" will not work this time.

Natural conservation requires living with *our planet, not* on *it.*

LEADERSHIP

In contrast to Western style government, the form of government with all *ali'i* at its head was subjective first and objective second. The success of a chosen *ali'i* member of Hawaiian society was contingent on his ability in having his people succeed in and celebrate life.

—*Patrick Ka'ano'i,* Hawaiian Writer

What if the purpose of government were to have everyone succeed in living life and celebrating life? What if one's success were seen as an ability to celebrate life and to facilitate others doing just that?

Leaders, then, would be chosen not on the basis of their ability to manipulate economic issues but because of their ability to envision and facilitate the living of life to its fullest.

When the purpose of government is to regulate and control, and government is based first on economics, celebrating life *may* be possible for a few, and even that is questionable.

❦

There are many views of leadership.

FREEDOM

Our people only took enough food for their immediate needs. When they woke in the morning, the children were told to go find breakfast. Hunting and gathering was a never-ending occupation. While this may have imposed some restrictions on them, their knowledge of their environment permitted a freedom seldom experienced by any other nation of people.

—Australian Aboriginal Wisdom

As I sit surrounded by "things," I have let it sink into me what it might mean to take only enough for my immediate needs. In reading and in being with tribal people, I have heard this philosophy again and again and I have tried to let myself comprehend it.

Intellectually, I understand the concept, *and* I came from a culture that has educated me to believe that my safety and security are somehow related to how much I have. The more labor-saving devices I have, the freer I am supposed to be.

Yet, when I am with Native people, I experience a freedom of the soul that money and things can't buy.

❧

It takes a lot of time and money to keep my labor-saving devices in top form.

LETTING GO OF RESENTMENTS

And he said when you get rid of that anger and resentment toward whites for what they have done, everything you ask with His name [the Creator] will come to you—no difficulty. Because you have built a compassion inside of you to the human race of the world. See, that is what they were talking about.

—*Eddie Box,* Ute Elder and Medicine Man
American Indian

Eddie Box is an Elder himself and he is speaking of what his Elders told him.

Only when we let go of our resentments can we become whole. This does not mean that people have not wronged us. Most of us have been wronged in one way or another. But when we begin to believe we are victims, we become filled with hate and resentment. Hate and resentment are like lightproof shades drawn on both sides of the room of the soul. They keep out the healing light of the Creator and they keep out the clarifying light of all our relations—humankind. Hate and resentment create a darkness in the soul that becomes progressively impenetrable.

Let others answer to their Higher Power for wrongs they have done. That's none of our business. Without our hate and resentments, we can again make contact with the Creator, and compassion will flow.

Healing starts with me.

WORK

All children had jobs to do. We worked alongside our old people.
—*Mihi Edwards,* Maori Writer

It's not just, "You do the dishes after dinner," or "You set the table," or "You take out the garbage." Those are chores.

I have noticed how much more my children are willing to pitch in when we work together.

In the circle of life, Native American people talk about going from childhood to youth to adulthood to old age, which again is childhood. What valuable time for children to work alongside the Elders! Elders have so much patience and so much to teach.

When children know that they are actually making a contribution to the welfare of their families, it's a wonderful way to build self-esteem! What an easy way of teaching each individual to do the jobs needed by society and become a part of the society. What a good way to learn the sacredness and the joy of work!

@

When we grow up working together, we learn the true meaning of work.

LOST CONNECTIONS

The White people got their way to understand. The Whiteman's way of learning things and going to school. But then you go back three or four hundred years and think about what their culture was. None of them living today understand it. The White people, too. So the old culture is not only lost with the Native people, it's also lost with the White people.

—*Peter John,* Athabaskan Elder and Chief
Minto, Alaska

What does it mean to be a people who have lost our culture? Since I have been spending so much time with Native people, this question has come to me again and again.

I know that Native people feel that it is essential to know one's roots, one's language, one's culture, and to be connected to the land of one's ancestors.

How has it affected those of us whose ancestors have wandered so far? If we are disconnected from our roots and culture, has this broken a felt connection with the earth that gives us the "knowing" of interconnectedness? Does it free us to use up and destroy because we no longer "know" our roots and connections? What do we have to learn about connectedness from Native people?

☯

What is lost when my culture and my roots are lost to me?

RELATIONSHIPS

During the first year a newly married couple discovers whether they can agree with each other and can be happy—if not, they part, and look for other partners. If we were to live together and disagree, we should be as foolish as the Whites.

—*Black Hawk,* Sauk Elder
American Indian

I had to chuckle at this one. The humor in some of these Elders' observations is delightful.

No "love at first sight" here. Relationships are to be tested, experienced, lived with, and grown into.

Romance or romance addiction, it appears, is an invention of Western culture. We hear a lot about love, beauty, sex, and attraction, but most of what we learn to get there is a subtle escape from intimacy.

Intimacy takes time. It doesn't happen, it grows, *and* if it doesn't grow, we can't make it happen.

☯

In a world aching for intimacy, we have a lot to learn about relationships.

MONEY/WORK

Money should never be a reward on its own. Love, a sense of accomplishment, and appreciation for one's work should always be foremost. We all play a part and contribute to the whole. . . . The work ethic of Hawai'i is one of personal excellence. The power that comes from one's personal excellence is *mana*. Money does not increase one's *mana*. . . . Hawai'i works for *mana*, the West works for money.

—*Patrick Ka'ano'i,* Hawaiian Writer

"Money should never be a reward on its own." "I want to be paid what I'm worth." Impossible in Hawaiian culture. "If I get paid more money, I'm worth more." Impossible in Hawaiian culture. "My identity and value come from what I do and how much money I make." Impossible in Hawaiian culture.

We hear so much, abstractly, about the value of work. Yet, work has lost its meaning. Workaholics are addicted to working, but almost all of them say that work has lost its essence.

In our culture, it sounds impossibly romantic to say that "we all play a part and contribute to the whole." Yet, there are many places on the planet that operate out of this belief, where one's power is in excellence.

☙

Money is not real. It is symbolic.

GUARDIAN SPIRITS

Kaitiaki or guardian spirits are left behind by deceased ancestors to watch over their descendants and to protect sacred places.

—*Cleve Barlow,* Maori Writer

I have often felt guarded and protected, but my theological training allowed for such phenomena only in the form of guardian angels. Then, at some point in my thinking, I begin to distinguish between who we pray to for daily help, guidance, and intervention, and what I think of as the only "real" prayer to God: "Thy will be done." It occurred to me that maybe who we pray to on a workaday basis are what my Maori friends call *Kaitiaki.*

What a comfort it is to know that I have guardian spirits who are active in my life! What a comfort to know that the sacred places on this planet are protected.

☯

Knowing the unseen . . . what a comfort!

WEALTH

Another point of importance is their children not being burden-some. In all the inquiries I made into the state of the poor, I found their happiness and ease generally relative to the number of their children, and nothing considered as such a misfortune as having none.

—*Arthur Young*
Writing about the Irish

Wealth is what we believe it to be. One of the major problems we have in this world is one culture's attempting to define what wealth is for another, or one culture's being willing to destroy the values of another in order to feed its own notion of wealth.

In so many places in the world, material possessions are not the criteria for happiness.

One Native American Elder told me that their wealth was the sound of their children's laughter as they played around the camp circle.

In so many places, children and Elders are considered to be the wealth of the people. Children offer so many opportunities for joy. The Irish have always valued children.

@9

Being poor can be defined in so many ways, as can wealth.

◄◦►◄◦►◄◦►◄◦►◄◦►◄◦►◄◦►◄◦►◄◦►◄◦►◄◦►◄◦►◄◦►◄◦►◄◦►

HOPE/LOOKING INSIDE

The real true self—the real pure heart—we can come together.
—*Franklin Kahn,* Navajo Elder
American Indian

In meeting with Elders, the one ever-present thread is—hope.

Franklin Kahn, like many Elders, is pained by what he sees happening to the earth and to his people and all people. He makes no bones about that. Yet, when he speaks, what I experience is not despair and futility—it is hope.

How can we find our real true self? We have to look inside. We have the answers in ourselves. We have to stop and take the time to rediscover our true selves. Maybe we believe that self has long since disappeared. Yet, in my experience—and in that of Franklin Kahn, I believe—I have never met anyone who has completely destroyed that true self—that living process—the connection with the Creator.

It may take work to return to our real, pure hearts, *and* it is possible.

◎◙

"We can come together." There is much hope in the promise.

GREED

And I don't understand why some people have more than others. People should share what they have. Greed is going to destroy everybody.

—*Derek Fowell,* Australian Writer

Greed is subtle. Most of us would not label ourselves greedy. It is a word applied to overdramatic characters in Shakespearean plays or people who aren't like us.

Yet, we can look closer. Greed can be keeping something we like but don't need when we know someone else would like to have it. Greed might be having an extra, just in case. Greed might be having one in every color. Greed might be believing that we own the land and everything on it. Greed might be having something to leave to our children. Greed may be not believing that God will provide.

@@

Greed is destructive, and it's something I need to look at.

WISDOM

A questioning man is halfway to being wise.

—Irish Proverb

"Don't just accept something because someone tells you it's so," my parents always said to me. "Check it out for yourself."

"Think for yourself" was a mantra in my house when I was growing up. In fact, my parents even encouraged me to question them and disagree when I saw fit. This did not mean that I did not respect them. I loved and respected them greatly, but they were the first to say that they could be wrong.

Questioning minds are the soul of a people. Eager, inquisitive minds are open to new information. Wisdom comes from openness.

☙❧

Closed minds and closed systems eventually devour themselves.

THE CIRCLE

You have noticed that everything an Indian does is in a circle, and that is because the Power of the World always works in circles, and everything tries to be round. The Wind, in its greatest power whirls. Birds make their nests in circles . . . the sun comes forth and goes down again in a circle. The Moon does the same, and both are round. The life of a man is a circle from childhood to childhood and so it is in everything where power moves.
   —*Hehaka Sapa (Black Elk)*, Oglala (Teton) Dakota Elder
   American Indian

The world is not linear. Life is not linear. Our understanding is limited when it is linear.

Native American wisdom always works in circles. Many people use the Medicine Wheel, which is a powerful teaching tool and way of understanding ourselves and our world. There are the four directions: north, south, east, and west. There are the four races: black, white, red, and yellow—all my relations moving together. There are the four cycles of life: the baby (child), the youth, the adult, and the elder, who returns to the child. There are the four parts of our being that need care: the physical, the emotional, the mental, and the spiritual. All are interconnected.

The universe is round. We come from the earth, it nourishes us even in our mother's womb, and we return to the earth.

☯

We view life differently when we think in circles.

A TIME OF URGENCY—A TIME TO LISTEN

Our planet was destroyed. When we came to this planet, our role was to protect this planet. We know what it means to have your planet destroyed.

—*Reuben Kelly,* Elder
Thainghetti People, Gurrigan Clan
Koorie [Australian Aboriginal]

Reuben Kelly is one of the most educated and intelligent men I know. He taught himself to read and write. He is well educated in Western thought and in Aboriginal myths, legends, and stories and in the Dreamtime. When he speaks, I listen carefully.

When Reuben Kelly talks about his planet being destroyed, he speaks with such quiet power and knowing that I have no question that he knows what he's talking about. His living concern about this planet, his feeling of urgency, and his conviction that white people have to listen, believe, and do something resonates deep in my being. I believe Reuben Kelly. I believe he knows and I believe we must do something together.

Listening has not been our strong suit in Western culture. We may need to develop some new skills.

LISTENING

Listen! Or your tongue will make you deaf.

—Cherokee Saying
American Indian

Being Irish, I am a great talker, and for years I believed that I had a lot of important things to say. These past few years, as I have been spending time with indigenous Elders, I find myself doing more and more listening. I learn so much when I listen.

Over the years, I have realized that there are four kinds of listening that are absolutely essential. I need to listen to myself. My culture had educated me not to listen to myself and even to try to ignore that there was a self to listen to.

I need to listen to other people, especially Elders. More and more I find myself hungry for what they have to say and the *way* they say it.

I need to listen to nature. Nature is one of my best teachers. My education tried to divorce me from nature, but, thank goodness, my mother would have none of that.

I need to listen to my God. I find my God in myself, in others, and in nature, and there is much more in listening to God. The universe has a voice I can hear, if my tongue has not made me deaf.

Listening takes time.

OWNERSHIP

The land was created by God. Therefore, it belongs to God.
—*Alex Pua,* Hawaiian Elder

Would anyone dispute this? The statement sounds so simple. Yet, we seem to have forgotten.

Every religion in the world recognizes some Creator. That seems universal. Yet, over time we seem to have assigned ownership—usually to ourselves.

Are we also created by God? Do we also, then, belong to God? Few would disagree. Yet, do we live our lives out of this knowing?

When we shift our perspectives and our values back to the simplicity of what we have always known, life becomes much simpler.

If the land belongs to God, I am just the custodian for a short time. I might lose my job if I don't do a good one, and remember who the owner is.

☯

Ownership is a matter of perspective!

◄O►◄O►◄O►◄O►◄O►◄O►◄O►◄O►◄O►◄O►◄O►◄O►◄O►◄O►◄O►◄O►◄O►

TALENTS

Each person is known to have a certain gift and certain ability, and is therefore able to make a contribution to the whole. There will be *tohunga*—the expert in bone carving; the expert in weaving, but there is in the *whanau* [extended family] a place for all.
—*Hiwi Tauroa,* Maori Writer

Imagine, what a productive society, what a safe society we would have if everyone had a place! In the *whanau* there is no such thing as handicapped—there is different—and each person who is different has her or his own particular gift to contribute. Children contribute what they can. They are not isolated from the decision making. Their gifts of inventiveness, creativity, joy, and energy are seen as contributions. People are not waiting for them to become adults. Groups are not segregated. Elders are persons with the greatest wisdom and therefore the best teachers because they carry the wisdom of the tribe and are patient.

It is the responsibility of the *whanau* to help find and bring out the special ability of everyone. Everyone *has* a place. No one has to *make* a place.

๛

God has given me my talents. All I have to do is use them.

RESPECT AND ACCEPTANCE

Many religions have been brought to this land. And the way my religion is, they teach me and taught me and told me to respect all religions. When someone else believes what his creator is, we can stand and pray together.

—*Horace Axtell,* Nez Percé Elder

When a religion is an open system, all other religions are valued and supported. When a religion believes that it is the only way, it also believes that it has to overpower and eradicate other systems to survive.

One of the questions I asked at the end of my book *Beyond Therapy, Beyond Science* was whether open systems could survive supporting other open and closed systems when the very focus of a closed system is to destroy open systems and anything unlike itself. If an open system tries to get rid of a closed system, it becomes a closed system. I believe that this is a major question facing the planet today.

I like the gentleness I hear when Horace Axtell speaks of respecting all religions. When others have belief, we can stand and pray together.

❧

I pray for a time when all religions respect one another—and the starting place is with me.

HEALING

Many hundreds of Hawaiians went to their graves with broken spirits, hearts laden with sadness, because of what Puritans obliterated with their black pall. Missionaries taught our people to bow their heads, close their eyes, clasp their hands and pray to their Lord. While the Hawaiians were busy learning to pray to the Christian God, his children were busy grabbing our land. They didn't let the right hand know what the left hand was doing. They bartered their souls for gold and traded their Lord for Hawaii. Now they have our country and we have Jehovah!

—*Mary Julia Glennie Bush*
Hawaiian Kupuna

An eloquent statement! Some people do not like to hear how Native people feel, and they are afraid it will be depressing. In my religious background, I was taught "you shall know the truth and the truth shall set you free." Even when painful, the truth is always healing. Dishonesty, even when done with the best of intentions, is destructive.

There is still a lot of Puritanism around. As one of my Hawaiian friends said, "The Hawaiians are dying from the missionary disease and the Hawaiians have become the missionaries. They live with shame and pain and suffering. They have ceased to be joyful in their bodies." How easy it is to take on the values of the oppressor.

We need to hear the hurt and anger of our whanau—*our human family—and heal together.*

WALKING

Walking is what I need to enjoy the most. Walking, you take in everything and enjoy the scenery.

—*Goodwin Semaken, Sr.,* Inupiat/Koyukon Elder
Kaltag, Alaska

Walking is not only good for the body, it is good for the soul. I loved reading this because sometimes I forget how much I love to walk, especially in the country. I get too busy, or it's not convenient, or I don't have the right shoes, or, or, or . . .

Walking, for me, is a way to notice. It is a way to be "in" nature and not just passing through it. Even in the city I see so much more if I walk.

@

It's important to remember—rushing is not walking.

MOVING ON

The spiritual ways have maintained us over time, especially through five hundred years of oppression.

The sun will come up. We have had five hundred years of building our strength as people and now we come into the spring.

—*Henrietta Mann, Ph.D.,* Southern Cheyenne Elder
American Indian

Many Native people believe they, like seeds through the winter, have been building their strength to come forth. Their legends have told them that the time would come when their knowledge and their wisdom would be needed by the planet. Many feel now is the time.

When we live life in such a way that we do not resent what has happened to us, but respect what we have experienced, we can learn from it. We can learn that it is our responsibility to do what we need to do to heal and to move on. We can become adults.

What I have experienced in my life is mine. It's up to me what I do with it.

PERSPECTIVE

My father used to tell us: "My children, whenever you have time, go and talk to your grandfather. He knows what our ancestors said." It was like a political discussion every time we talked to him, whereby he'd tell us about his life, his own grandparents' lives, and something of the lives of those who'd lived before them. He'd explain why our people didn't live as long now as our ancestors did. He said that when he was a boy, he saw people of a hundred and fifteen, a hundred and seventeen, still alive. He said: "It's not you children's fault. The modern machines which have come to our land are to blame." You have to remember of course, that my grandfather never went to school. But he'd say: "It's that you eat these chemical things today and that stops you living as long as you should. It's not your fault but that's how it is."

—*Rigoberta Menchú*, Quiché Indian
Guatemala

Listen to the Elders. Learn from the Elders. They have a perspective that is age tested and they have listened to their Elders, who listened to *theirs*.

In order to see what we have created, we have to get out of it enough so that we can have some perspective. The Elders offer us that perspective.

❧

We have to get back into health again and we need help to get perspective.

<<o><o><o><o><o><o><o><o><o><o><o><o><o><o><o><o><o><o><o>>

GRATITUDE

[On farming] For me, there was always a sense of contentment in feeling a rhythm beneath my feet. The heartbeat of the land. That season would follow season and that the rhythm would never alter. Knowing this brought me peace like no other I had known.
—*Witi Ihimaera,* Maori Writer

I have, on occasion, known deep within me a feeling of being in rhythm with the heartbeat of the land and even with the heartbeat of the universe. At those times, there is such a peace and oneness that all else seems insignificant. I realize at those times that this must be what is meant by the "peace that passeth all understanding."

There is so much to trust and so much to be grateful for: that season will follow season; that the sun will come; that the stars will be in the sky. Sometimes I forget the things I can count on and I try to make those I can't count on reliable.

๏๏

I am grateful for the peace that is mine.

HERITAGE

Without heritage ... without lands ... without nations ...
You'll just be another millionaire.

—*Oren Lyons,* Onondaga Tribal Chief
American Indian

Oren Lyons is one sharp fellow. He not only has a way with words, he has a way with ideas. In just a few words, he gives us the essence of two very different worldviews.

I need to know who I am and where I come from. I need to know that I do not live my life in isolation. I need to know that I have the blood of my ancestors in my veins, the wisdom of the Elders in my brain, and the truth of my Creator in my soul. Without this heritage, I am alone.

I need to have my place to stand. This does not mean that I need to own land necessarily to have my place. As we expand in our awareness, the planet becomes our place to stand.

And I need to have a community, a nation, that shares my knowledge, heritage, and worldview. I need to be connected.

What good is money? It can never tell us who we are, why we're here, where we came from, and to whom we belong.

◉◉

Why settle for money?

ADDICTION

By the time I left school I had already experienced racism at its worst, being banned from access to the local swimming pool and being relegated to the black-only front three rows downstairs at the local picture theatre. When I was hospitalized after a football injury I found myself in the black ward at Kempsey Hospital. Over the years I saw many of my friends and family turn to alcohol as an escape from the pain of their existence and, at the age of 15, I made the decision never to drink alcohol or smoke cigarettes—both major agents of genocide—a golden rule I have followed throughout my life.

—*Burnum Burnum*
Australian Aboriginal Writer

Native people can tell us a lot about the genocide caused by drugs, cigarettes, and alcohol. In Western culture, we seem reluctant to admit that addiction is a major societal issue. Of course, denial is a major cornerstone of the disease.

Native people are outspoken and clear about the effects of addiction—not only on individuals but on the entire culture. We have something to learn here.

☯

Addicts always believe they are not being destroyed by their addiction.

CARING FOR THE ENVIRONMENT

We need to care for the environment the way we care for our children.

—Hawaiian Native Elder

Hawaiians love their children! They have a saying: *"He lei poina 'ole ke keiki."* (A lei never forgotten is the beloved child.) Children are seen as the beloved flowers of Hawaii. They bring joy and beauty to the land. Children in Hawaii are the result of our loving one another, and they are nurtured, valued, treasured, and loved.

Historically and even today, when a Hawaiian family is childless, children are literally given to them as the most precious blossoms to be shared.

In a land that values children so much, it is very important to suggest that we give that same kind of tenderness and love to the environment.

We need to cradle the environment. We need to nurture it. We need to pamper it. We need to live *with* it.

❧

In caring for the environment, we care for the children of our future. The children are our future.

TRUST

They always told us to share food, even if it's our last. Never let anyone leave our home without a meal. Never make bad feelings over food, because food comes along every day.

—*Clara Honea*, Athabaskan Elder
Ruby, Alaska

Sharing is something that is stressed in every tribal society. In the life that Clara Honea was talking about, food was the issue of the day. Her people lived as what the modern world calls a subsistence society. It was not a materialistic society. Yet, the sharing of food was the basic value. No one was ever to leave their house without a meal.

What I like so much about her statement is the last phrase, "because food comes along every day." There is so much in this statement. Food is precious and important and even hard to come by, *and* there is a quiet assurance that it will come. Just as the seasons will come.

Why would we ever not share what we have with our friends when we trust the cycle of life?

◎

What I need comes along. I have to do my footwork and I do get what I need.

SPIRITUALITY

I want all my children and grandchildren to experience some part of the spiritual, Indian spiritual beliefs.

—*Andrea Axtell,* Nez Percé Elder
American Indian

Andrea Axtell is a Nez Percé Elder. Her children are well educated and hold jobs in the white world. Other than overworking and rushing all the time, there's no problem with that. Yet, they and Andrea have come to know that they need to reconnect with their Indian spiritual beliefs. There is something there that is not satisfied by success in the white world or by white religion.

How good it is to go where our spirit leads us. To go to a spirituality that satisfies us! We are spiritual beings and our inner being has a knowing that transcends all cultures and times.

It is the job of the soul to seek out what feeds it.

❧

When my soul is fed, I am whole.

DIVERSITY

The Aboriginal Christians are convinced and believe that the God of the Bible was with us and our people in the Dreamtime. He was very active in our history. He has come to us in many different ways and many different forms to reveal his presence. He spoke to us through his creation, the beauty of the nature that clothes itself in God's glory that convinced us and made us believe that he is also the God of the Aboriginal race in Australia.

Our Aboriginality is God's given gift to us as people, of which we are very proud.

—*The Reverend Djiniyini Gondarra*
Australian Aboriginal Writer

What a statement of faith! According to the Aboriginal Elders with whom I have spoken, their myths and legends told them that a people would come who would teach them of a powerful spiritual leader. Christianity is no problem for them. They only have a problem with a closed-system Christianity that does not leave room for God having created Aboriginals as people of God.

If God is the God of Creation, then that God has created the wondrous differences that exist on this planet. This diversity must be here for a reason.

Would a tunnel-visioned God have created a wide-spectrum world?

DECEMBER

OBSERVATION AND WONDER

Observation was certain to have its rewards. Interest, wonder, admiration grew, and the fact was appreciated that life was more than mere human manifestation; it was expressed in a multitude of forms.

> —*Chief Luther Standing Bear,* Oglala (Teton) Sioux Elder
>   American Indian

Observe all the life around us, especially nature, which offers us an endless source of learning. When we know that we are only one part of a much larger scheme of things, we can learn what we need to know by putting ourselves in proper perspective with life around us.

I remember having an especially difficult time with a "weed" that was growing in my yard and strangling other plants that I had carefully nurtured. It appeared quite unexpectedly after a hurricane. At first, I attacked it head-on and started to tear it out of my ti trees. And in so doing, I destroyed the precious ti leaves. Every day for several months I worked with this vine in my yard (it grows very fast!)

I began to see that it was like some people I know and had many of the same frightening characteristics. I also saw it helping to restore the forest after the hurricane by breaking down dead trees. I saw that my immediate impulse to demolish it actually destroyed what I was trying to protect—I was responding out of a perspective of a closed system. I learned that I had a lot more to learn about this plant *and* myself.

When I move from struggle and control to observation and wonder, I begin to learn.

FORGIVENESS

For instance, like you, you have been involved in this movement of kind of a feeling that you've been hurt. But, there it is, you've got to get rid of that first. This is very difficult.

They said to be good to each other. Now here is what those are healing for all of us, especially young people. They say be good even to the white man. Our grandfathers said that. Are we going to be good to the white man after what they have done to us?

Some people would think, NO! They think, look what they did to our tribe. But, who's telling you? Grandfather is telling you to do that! That was the test for us being Indian people.

—*Eddie Box,* Ute Elder and Medicine Man
American Indian

Listening to the wisdom of the Grandfathers is a big part of what it means to be Indian. If a people who have been wronged (no treaty made by the American government with American Indians was ever kept) are being told to forgive and be good to white people, what is it we need to do?

We can learn forgiveness. We can learn to look at the wisdom of seeing the broader picture. We can reach back to the hands that are reaching out to us.

☯

Forgiveness starts with the self.

RECEIVING

"Tienes que aprender a recibir el nene."

I was practicing as a naturopath in my small clinic in one room of my two-room home in Solola, Guatemala, 1973. I knew midwifery was next. My midwife and I were the only ones present at my son's birth that same year. She had arrived just in time to catch him. It was, and remains, the most precious moment of my life. I knew I had more karma with that. I had spoken with my neighbors about the local *comadrona*. One day I was walking back from market with my son, Dov, on my back and she approached me. She was tiny, maybe 4 feet 8 inches, thin, her unwrinkled skin tight across her high cheekbones, her grey hair in thin braids, and her sparkling black eyes meeting mine. She wore *traje* [traditional woven Mayan dress] from Solola. We were the only people on the path. An ancient *comadrona* and a gringa medicine woman. An odd couple.

Without an introduction, she grabbed me with her eyes and said, *"Tienes que aprender a recibir el nene."* You will learn to receive the baby. (Not deliver, but Receive!) And that's what we spent the next two and one half years doing together.

— As told by *Latifa Amdur,* L.Ac, Dipl. Ac., and C.H.
Guatemala

Learning to receive. We receive a baby. We don't deliver it. We receive the gifts of the Creator. We don't make them happen. We receive love, we can't make people love us.

❧

When we risk learning to receive, we risk getting what we want.

DIFFERENCES/DIVERSITY

One important belief is that Io Matua has given a unique heritage to each and every culture across the world. No culture is more or less important than another—to suggest that there is, is to criticize the Creator.

—*Rangimarie Turuki Pere,* Maori Writer

How often I have thoughts and feelings that "criticize the Creator." All the "isms" are criti*cisms* of the Creator. How subtle they are.

This Maori writer reminds us of the beauty and necessity of diversity. When was it that human beings began to see themselves as the end point of evolution? And when was it that certain human beings began to see themselves and their culture as more evolved?

Nature teaches the necessity of diversity. The Creator has created diversity. Was that a mistake?

When we see ourselves as participating in an ongoing creative process, we recognize that diversity and differences are essential for survival.

❦

Who are we to think we know it all?

OPEN SYSTEMS

It is a time to listen to Aboriginal people. It is a time to appreciate our spirituality, to hear our cries and see our oppression, and to share in it. It is time to respect and honour our spirituality completely and without reservation—just as we are willing to respect your roots.

—*The Reverend Djiniyini Gondarra*
Australian Aboriginal Writer

What a clear statement! It is time for us to listen to and learn from those we considered our inferiors.

It is time to deal with oppression on a global level, to forgive ourselves when we have been oppressors in the past, and to make our amends by living our lives in a new way today.

It is time to look at closed systems. Closed systems are the root of oppression. Closed systems exist to destroy everything unlike themselves. We and only we can stop and admit how we perpetuate closed systems in our lives.

The Australian Aboriginals are asking us to become an open system with them. They are asking us to respect and value the differences between us, to let go of our cultural arrogance and to respect their spirituality. The invitation has been given.

☙❧

Open systems are a lot of fun.

◆◇◆◇◆◇◆◇◆◇◆◇◆◇◆◇◆◇◆◇◆◇◆◇◆◇◆◇◆◇◆◇◆◇◆

POSSESSIONS

It was our belief that love of possessions is a weakness to be over-come. Its appeal is to the material part, and if allowed its way, it will in time disturb one's spiritual balance. Therefore, children must early learn the beauty of generosity. They are taught to give what they prize most, that they may taste the happiness of giving.

—*Ohiyesa (Charles Eastman)*
Santee Sioux Writer and Elder
American Indian

The American dream is to have. Very early, we teach our children what is "theirs" and not to take other people's things. From an early age, we model attachment. The American Indians teach their children to give up what they love the most. These are two very different systems. It is easy to see how the former system could take advantage of the latter—in terms of things and possessions.

And the American Indians are warning us that this way of being in the world will disturb our spiritual balance. Are we a people whose spiritual balance has been disturbed? Only we can answer.

೧௦

Is there something I have that is more important to me than my spirituality? If so, I need to take a look.

SPIRITUAL LIVING

> That Ireland which we dreamed of would be the home of a people who valued material wealth only as the basis for right living, of a people who were satisfied with frugal comfort and devoted their leisure to the things of the spirit.
>
> —*Éamon De Valera,* Irish Politician

This is a politician speaking. Imagine a country satisfied with "frugal comfort" as a basis for "right living" and a vision of devoting their "leisure to things of the spirit."

I was touched by this segment of De Valera's speech because these values touch the Irish heritage I know and the Ireland I know today.

The spiritual is everyday among my Irish friends. Church and Mass are very much part of religion, and the practical and inherited spirituality of the land goes far beyond simple religion. There is still a deep feeling for spirituality in Ireland.

൭൦

We have something to learn about "frugal comfort" and devoting our "leisure to the things of the spirit."

GRATITUDE

The release that my family is finding is going back to the spiritual ways. We have a longhouse. We don't have services, it isn't like a set service where you go in there at ten and you're out by eleven. It's just a process where we all get together. I can remember back in the old days, my young days. We're not in a hurry. That's everybody's problem, we go and sit and visit. Then we sing our songs and then we'll eat our traditional foods. Every time we get together, we thank the Creator for water, salmon, our venison, and our roots, our berries, and then we'll sing and thank again. Thank the water again, without the water we could not exist. Then afterward, we sit and visit again.

—*Andrea Axtell,* Nez Percé Elder
American Indian

When Andrea Axtell talks about going back to her spiritual ways, she is talking about a spirituality that is all-encompassing, based in community and in process. Gratitude is important in this spirituality. We have so much to be grateful for as we live our lives, and sharing gratitude makes it so much more meaningful.

The spirituality that Andrea Axtell shares is not bound by form. It is enriched by process.

◎

Gratitude is not static. It is an ever-flowing river.

CHANGE

As we walk along the trail of life we carry a bowl and each experience we have is like a stone we pick up and put into the bowl. To change all we have to do is turn the bowl upside down and then show our light there.

—*Alex Pua,* Hawaiian Elder

Western psychology tells us that we have scars from what has been done to us that will never heal, and therefore we are victims who may need support all our lives. Native cultures tell us that we have had experiences and it is up to us what we do with those experiences. We have the power to heal within us. And if we are willing to do our work, not to focus blame on others, to give up being a "victim," to do what we must to work through our feelings about what has happened to us, then we can take responsibility for our lives. It is not a matter of will, it is a matter of working with our Creator to become all we can be—to live our lives.

All we have to do is to be willing to turn the bowl over and heal. Then our light can show.

❦

I am responsible for my life—not to blame—responsible. Only I can choose to live it.

WE HAVE WHAT WE NEED

So, I would say right off the bat, that if we're going to change, make changes, the first thing that we have to do is understand discipline. Then being able to apply it to ourselves individually. Because only individually can we change things. We can't go out and tell somebody else what to do. But, first we have to do it ourselves.

—*Phil Lane, Sr.,* Yankton Lakota Elder
American Indian

The only person we can change is ourself. We hear this again and again from Native Americans. "We can't go out and tell somebody else what to do." The Elders I know are perfectly willing to share their knowledge and information with anyone who is willing to learn and they will never tell anyone what to do. Out of respect, that is left to the individual. No American Indian Elder would presume to know what another needs. They are experts in sharing the knowledge of the ancestors and the tribe. Their belief that the Creator has placed in each of us what we need to know to live a full, happy, and spiritual life is so deep that they would never presume to assume. Respect for individuals and their finding their way is complete.

◎◎

It is not only what the Elders say, it is also the way they say it and what they do with what they say that gives such wisdom.

COMMUNITY

Another time we were in the *mercado* [marketplace]. All the people come into town on market day and bring their vegetables, fruits, material, herbs, hardware, incense, pots, pans, firewood, anything and everything. People come from the town center and all the surrounding area to buy, to sell, to connect, to gossip. It's the television, the newspaper, the coffee house, the meeting place. The *abuelita* [little grandmother] and I were together and I asked her how many babies she had received in her sixty-four years of midwifery. She spent a few poignant moments looking over the throng, the enormous abundance of humanity and wares. Then she looked at me and replied, *"¡Pues, todo el Pueblo!"* [Well, the whole village!]
— As told to me by *Latifa Amdur*, L. Ac, Dipl. Ac., and C.H.
Guatemala

Latifa goes on to say that the word *pueblo* "is one of those words that is uniquely Spanish. It literally means something like 'all the beings who encompass this village, all who make it what it is, all who give it its identity.'"

She further states, "It has always amazed me to think that anyone sixty-four years or under had been guided into the world by the wonderful tiny brown hands of my *abuelita*."

◎◎

In community, we live and work together. There is no hierarchy of profession.

RESPECT

A lot of our kids—I say you think you are an Indian just because you wear red bandanna or war dance. Not being Indian. Have to respect yourself, others, Elders, and everybody else. Then you are an Indian.

—*Jeanette Timentwa,* Colville Lake Tribe Elder
American Indian

Jeanette Timentwa is one of my favorite people. She doesn't mince words and she never misses a chance to get money for projects with "her kids." She has worked wonders with many Indian kids who were in trouble by teaching them the "old way" and the old spirituality. Her kids know the meaning of respect.

Respect is a word that I find on my lips more and more in the last few years. Respect who I am and why the Creator has put me here. Respect others and the path they need to take. Respect differences and learn from them. Respect the Elders and let their wisdom in. Respect all life and know that I am one with it. Respect all people and know that we have the same Creator who has given us the pool of talents we need for this planet. Respect our interconnectedness and our oneness. Respect nature. Respect life.

Respect is a very versatile attitude. It can be applied to so many things.

BIRTHING

"When you smoke little babies and mothers, you are part of a special ceremony—like men have special law, women have special law and ways too for smoking babies."

Borning by the Grandmothers' Law is a process guided by rites and skills, an oral tradition passed down through successive generations by experience. Aboriginal women have control over their own lives, bodies and babies in this borning process. Few tools are needed and helping hands are used for support and massage.

—From the Congress Alukura, 1990
Australian Aboriginal Women's Council

Birthing is one of the most important rites of passage. Everyone who has given birth or has participated in a birthing knows that it is a process that transcends linear time. It is pure Living the Process.

Times like these are sacred, and technology is not the issue. Times like these are our opportunity to participate in the process of life at its deepest level.

We have much to learn from the Grandmothers' Law about birthing. Our fears have removed us from our bodies and left us with a lonely and sterile approach to birth. I know that I certainly could have used support, massage, and the wisdom of the Grandmothers when I was birthing.

❧

The wisdom the Grandmothers bring to birthing is everyday wisdom. It is not just for special occasions.

WE ARE RESPONSIBLE FOR HOW
OUR TONGUE WAGS

Heri kukwaa kidole kuliko kukwaa Ulimi.

Better to stumble with the toe than with the tongue.

—Swahili Proverb

There are so many Native proverbs about being responsible for what comes out of our mouths.

We can take truth-speaking seriously and, as far as we are able, never lie to ourselves or anyone else. It's just not worth it.

We can also take a good look at our judgmentalism. If we're speaking out of judgment, we had better be quiet.

Interpretation is another, rather subtle form of judgmentalism—one that shows a lack of respect for others. Interpretation is supported and accepted in our society, and this doesn't mean that it's necessarily helpful.

Anger is a good, clean, healthy emotion. And rarely, if ever, is it appropriate to direct it at others. We need to learn safe ways to honor and process our anger. Puking it onto others only does harm.

◉

When I stumble with the toe, I fall down. When I stumble with the tongue, I invite disaster.

YES! I want to SAVE $20 on RoadCare™ and receive my FREE 35mm Panorama Camera.

Name _____

Address_____ Lot/Apt#_____

City_____ State ____ Zip _____

Phone (___) _____

AMOUNT $_____
- ☐ Check or Money Order
- ☐ MasterCard ☐ Visa
- ☐ American Express
- ☐ Discover ☐ Diners Club

Charge Card #

Exp. Date

12 Month Coverage
☐ **President's Club Price –**
Only ~~$99~~ **$79**

For Instant Enrollment Call 1-800-828-4258 or Mail This Form to:

Camping World RoadCare™
4040 Mystic Valley Parkway
Boston, MA 02155-6918

Offer Expires July 31, 1996.   Code: C6450

Yours FREE when
Camping World's Roa
Road Servic

THE WISDOM OF THE ELDERS

The Elders once told me that the Indian people were spared so that we can be the driving force to save Mother Earth. The ashes of our ancestors have been intermingled with the earth on this continent for millennia.

—*Billy Redwing Toyac*, Piscataway Chief
American Indian

Many Native people have been told this by their Elders. This message of coming faith to save the planet is in myths, legends, and stories of Native people the world over. For hundreds of years, they have held this information close to their hearts and now is the time they have been told they are to share it.

This sharing is like a wave that has been building throughout many generations. They are choosing messengers to share the information. All who read this book are, in a way, chosen to receive this message because it has been encouraged and blessed by the contributing Elders.

Only those who continue to have a close relationship with Mother Earth will know how to save her.

☯

It's time to listen to the wisdom of the Elders.

GOD AS ALL

God . . . was in the food they ate, in the water they drank, in the air they breathed, in the earth they trod on and died on, in the words they spoke, in the sleep they slept and the dreams they dreamt, in the everywhere and the everything.
— *Albert Wendt,* Samoan Writer

Some Pacific cultures don't even have a word for God. This is not because God isn't there. It's because God is assumed. God is self-evident. God is so present that there is no need for a term because God is life itself.

I wonder when we as a species divided ourselves from the life force so deeply that we had to develop a concept of God as something separate from ourselves?

☯

The God of everywhere and everything is always with me.

◄○►◄○►◄○►◄○►◄○►◄○►◄○►◄○►◄○►◄○►◄○►◄○►◄○►◄○►◄○►◄○►◄○►

TAKING MY PLACE

It takes every blade of grass to make the meadow green.
—Irish Proverb

Each of us is important in the scheme of things. None of us is "too much" or is here accidentally. No one else is who I am. Only I can be who I am, and I can spend my life trying to be who I am. And I am who I am. For the meadow to be green, I have to accept taking my place as a blade of grass and growing as green as I can. I may want to be a flower or a tree, and I have my part to play as a blade of grass.

There are no mistakes—only my refusal to be who I am. I am important in the scheme of things.

☯

There is nothing more beautiful than a green Irish meadow.

RESPONSIBILITY

While living I want to live well. I know I have to die sometime, but even if the heavens were to fall on me, I want to do what is right. There is one God looking down on us all. We are all children of the one God. God is listening to me. The sun, the darkness, the winds, are listening to what we now say.

—*Geronimo,* Chiricahua Apache Warrior
American Indian

Geronimo was a brilliant man. He was also a very spiritual man. His story is worth knowing.

I was inspired as I read his words. The first sentence took a lot of "sitting with." Just what is "living well" in this day and age? More and more for me it has become just quietly living my spirituality, living my process—wanting to do what is right—listening to that gyroscope inside myself that links me to all knowing. When I feel that inner clarity, I know what right living is.

When I know that "God is listening to me," and I know that "the sun, the darkness, the winds, are listening to what I now say," I pray to speak the wisdom in truth as I know it.

I am responsible for what I say. I am responsible for how I choose to live my life. My life is what I do with it.

BELONGING HERE

You always have your place. Every person in the tribe has her or his place and no one else can take your place. You may go away for a month, a year, thirty years—and when you come back your place is always there.

—Australian Aboriginal Elder

As I listened to the Australian Aboriginal Elders talk about always having our place, I felt shivers up and down my spine. I thought of all the people I know who feel they have to achieve in order to have a place or that they have to make a place for themselves in their family and it never quite happens.

I thought of the confidence and self-esteem that are "givens" when we know that we "belong."

I thought of how many years I spent feeling like an outsider and not really knowing what I had to do to be an "insider" until I learned that all those who looked like insiders were feeling like outsiders too. I called this my "inclusion issue."

I began to see how difficult it is to "belong" in a society built on competition, comparison, and escape from intimacy.

❧

Belonging is a cultural issue as well as an individual issue. Being in community helps a lot.

KNOWLEDGE

Mwana mugimu: ava ku ngozi.

A strong healthy child: is already strong when carried in the cloth on the back of the mother.

—Ugandan Proverb

A Ugandan friend told me this proverb. He and his colleagues had used it as the name of the well-baby clinic they ran in Uganda for Native women and their children.

He shared with me how the proverb means that if the baby is already carried on the back, it has passed the crisis of birth and the dangers of neonatal life. Ugandans use a play on words here, too. The word for "sack"—the "sack" the mother carries the baby in— can also mean the sac in the uterus that the mother holds the baby in. So if the mother is healthy, the baby has a healthy start.

His eyes gleamed with excitement when he shared how their work was built on the women sharing their knowledge rather than outside authorities coming and telling them what they should do.

ᕬᕟᕒ

The best knowledge comes from inside.

AROHA

Aroha is:
   Unconditional love that is derived from the presence and breath of the Creator.

   Aroha is an important concept in regard to the survival and true strength of *whanaungatanga* [kinship ties, extended family across the universe]. It is a quality that is essential to the survival and total well-being of the world community. It is a pillar of life from *Io Matua* [the Godhead, the Divine Parent].

   Aroha is not to be talked about, it is only meaningful when actioned.

—*Rangimarie Turuki Pere,* Maori Writer

"Unconditional love that is derived from the breath of the Creator." I have known *aroha* and I have given *aroha.* I know it when I feel it.

Often, in the places where unconditional love is talked about, I don't feel it. Perhaps if it is happening, we don't have to talk about it. I don't want to talk about it here. And I do know we have something here to learn from Native people, and I know that the planet needs *aroha.*

ꩰ

I can't make aroha *happen. I can be open to it and look for the blocks in me that prevent my giving and receiving it.*

NATURE AS TEACHER

Nature is God's greatest teacher. Man must learn to attune his higher spiritual consciousness to the harmonious flow of nature and feel the throbbing heartbeat of the Man [sic] in heaven who created it for lasting duration in order to realize his oneness with nature and with God.

—Old Native Hawaiian Fisherman

Nature is my greatest teacher. When I take the time to go into nature, it takes me a while to settle down to the rhythm of my surroundings. Initially, what I hear is the rushing of my own heart and the pounding of my brain. It takes me a while to leave my culture behind me and begin to attune to the "harmonious flow of nature." I make a commitment to take as long as I need to slow down and listen.

God's messages in nature do not just enter the brain, they enter the whole being and move into a flow of consciousness that assures us of the oneness of all things with the Creator.

Only when my body and brain slow down enough do I have the possibility to know oneness.

◉◉

My "higher spiritual consciousness" is present in my oneness with nature. I have but to wait with it.

LISTENING/LEARNING/RESPECT

My father used to say: "There are many secrets we must not tell. We must keep our secrets." He said that no rich man, no landowner, no priest, or nun, must ever know our secrets. If we don't protect our ancestors' secrets, we'll be responsible for killing them.

—*Rigoberta Menchú,* Quiché Indian
Guatemala

I have heard so much about getting the "secrets" of Native people. So many people want to become a shaman or learn the rituals and ceremonies. I have even heard of people paying to steal the secrets of Australian Aboriginals. And wherever I have contact with indigenous people, I hear them say what Rigoberta Menchú's father said: "Don't give away our secrets."

I find this eagerness to acquire Native secrets very strange. It is clear to me that we cannot plug in the rituals and secrets mechanically and make them work. They come out of a culture and are perpetuators of that culture. Others can never fully understand that cultural context.

I find it a privilege to learn whatever those of other cultures want to share with me. Whatever is shared is more than enough to challenge me and push me to new vistas.

The wisdom of Native people can open many new doors to spirituality. I am grateful for whatever Native people have to share with me.

‣◦◄‣◦◄‣◦◄‣◦◄‣◦◄‣◦◄‣◦◄‣◦◄‣◦◄‣◦◄‣◦◄‣◦◄‣◦◄‣◦◄‣◦◄‣◦◄‣◦◄

COMMUNITY

Even a man with a hundred horses may need to ask another for a whip.

—Ladakhi Saying

The Ladakhi culture is built on community, interconnectedness, and mutual support, along with a living knowledge that they are part of an eternal flow of the universe that is greater than each person. Security and self-respect are related to belonging to their place on the earth and in the community.

Healthy individuals and societies are those in which each person knows that she or he has a particular place and where mutual interdependence in community results in freedom and independence.

We can learn from the Ladakhi knowing and experience of community. I live in community. Mine is an interrelated worldwide community in which people take responsibility for themselves and their natural ability to heal while also offering mutual support for one another.

In community, our very interdependence gives us freedom. Freedom grants security and security brings joy and support for others.

I may own much more than I need, and still, what I really need is my community.

❂

Community is the playground where we can move through the dance of life.

ACHIEVEMENT

In Europe, as people developed their civilisation from the caves to the cathedrals, they left clear evidence of their achievement for future generations to admire. In Australia, the land itself is the cathedral and worship is not confined to any four walls. Each step is a prayer and every form in the landscape—and everything that moves in it—were put there specifically for the people to use and manage. And the mythic beings made clear the responsibility of the people in preserving and nurturing the environment. Their success in managing their world so successfully, and sustaining their culture for so long, is now attracting the worldwide respect it deserves.

—*Burnum Burnum*
Australian Aboriginal Writer

We have something to learn here. Western culture has used the resources of the earth to try to improve upon the creations of God. We may claim that our works are inspired by God, yet they were conceived, designed, and built by people.

How would we live differently if we saw ourselves as custodians of our place? I like the idea of every step being a prayer. I know that when I am in tune with myself and my Living Process, life becomes a prayer. There is no separation between what I am doing and my spirituality. I felt this among the Aboriginals in Australia and I sense that it has much to do with the way they live with their place.

◎◎

I can achieve nothing greater than to live my life in tune with the Creator and to leave a better place for those who follow.

INTIMACY

I am more than my father's son. For these people I am son, friend, father too. They are to me in turn, my sons, daughters, fathers and mothers. That is the Maori way: not to talk of one family for we belong to each other, not only family living but family dead.

—*Witi Ihimaera*, Maori Writer

Relationships are not that simple. We have tried to make them one-dimensional and linear. Our illusion is that relating in this way gives more control, but does it give life?

Participating in relationships in a Maori *whanau* (extended family) has a feeling of texture to it. There is none of the illusion of security that rigidity feeds. Rather, there is the security and freedom that comes with participating in an ever-changing kaleidoscope of a moving process where one belongs. Security does not come from having things "nailed down." Security comes from knowing that one always has a place in the movement and the changing.

When we can no longer hide behind a role, we are pushed to present ourselves and then run the risk of real intimacy.

Intimacy, real intimacy, is always out of control.

COMMUNITY

Each individual is supported by a web of intimate relationships, and no one relationship has to bear too much weight. In Ladakh, I have never observed anything approaching the needy attachment or the guilt and rejection that is so characteristic of the nuclear family. All the signs tell us that the nuclear family is not working.

> —*Helena Norberg-Hodge,* writing about the Ladakh

While our Western governments and religious structures are pushing for more support for the nuclear family, many individuals are realizing that the nuclear family can never meet the needs of its individuals. Some are even beginning to wonder why our societal structures keep pushing for a model that produces damaged individuals.

Native people the world over look at our nuclear families with amazement and sadness—amazement that we do not know this structure does not work well, and sadness for the many individuals who are not getting their needs met.

We are now faced with the possibility of admitting that we need a broader base of support and letting Native people teach us about larger community support systems.

☯

Community is not something we can "make" happen. Community emerges as we participate in life with those around us.

STORIES

I try to share my grandfather's stories and knowledge. He often said "share all stories, it beautifies Mother Earth, especially in different voices. It's bad if all stories become one, there's no more stories, no more life."

—*Lupita Johnson,* Navajo Park Ranger
American Indian

Hearing stories, hearing diversity, hearing from those unlike ourselves. Who knows what we get from just hearing the stories? Sometimes our brains think we need to pull out the lesson and categorize it, and maybe the important thing is just hearing the story.

Here is one story I liked a lot from an Australian Aboriginal woman named Kukika:

I used to see my grandmother, for my sake she used to carry this lovely little *piti*, this lovely dainty little bowl, for my sake. In that little *piti* she used to have grass, in that *piti*, to save that water inside. She used to make me sit down, looking after this water when she go out hunting. And I used to sit down, wait. What time my Nanna gonna come back? I used to sit down, wait, wait. Then, see a dog coming first, her pet dog. When I see that dog I get happy, know that my Nanna is coming back home. I was about—must be about ten years old when my Nanna taught me bush life.

✺

Hearing stories grounds us—the more stories, the better; the greater the diversity, the better.

WORDS OF WISDOM

Whilst feeling compassion for you in the sweetness of our repose, we wonder at the anxieties and cares which you give yourselves, night and day.

—Gaspesian (Micmac) Chief
Canada

This was said over three hundred years ago by a Canadian Indian chief observing Europeans. I am struck by how timely the words are today. In spite of our modern conveniences and the belief that technology would give us so much leisure time that it would be a problem, we are finding that just the opposite is true. In general, "civilized" (white) people have much less time for the "sweetness of our repose." In fact, we find that anxiety and stress are the "gifts of modern science and modern living."

What have we to learn from the words of the old Indian chief? If these anxieties and cares are something we give ourselves, then we must also have the choice of *not* giving them to ourselves.

❧

Listen, listen, listen. We have much to learn.

CELEBRATION

Might I behold thee, Might I know thee, Might I consider thee,
Might I understand thee, O Lord of the universe.

—Inca Song
South America

I have the possibility, the sacred possibility, of knowing thee and thy ways.

I have the possibility of living in tune with all Creation.

I have the possibility of knowing and respecting the diversity of all Creation.

I have the possibility of living the oneness and interconnectedness of all Creation.

I have the possibility of living the circle of life.

I have the possibility of looking inside to find the answers that the Creator has given me.

I have the possibility of accepting my life and my mistakes as gifts from my Creator.

I have the possibility of seeing the Lord of the universe in nature and in the diversity of Creation.

I have the possibility of being one with the universe.

෨෨

All life is a celebration of the Creator.

◄◦►◄◦►◄◦►◄◦►◄◦►◄◦►◄◦►◄◦►◄◦►◄◦►◄◦►◄◦►◄◦►◄◦►◄◦►◄◦►◄◦►

THERE IS STILL TIME

From the beginning of their activity in the islands, the mission-aries clashed with the *tahunas* [priests, adepts, skilled practitioners] who were enlightened teachers of the former Hawai'ian priest-hood. They thereby cut themselves off from the supply line of ancient wisdom.

—*Leinani Melville,* Hawaiian Kupuna

We still have the opportunity to open ourselves up to the "supply line of ancient wisdom." Although Western culture has tried to suppress this wisdom, miraculously, it is still there.

Native people the world over are coming forth and offering their wisdom to those who are willing and able to hear. We don't have to seek it out, fight for it, or steal it. This wisdom is being freely of-fered. In return, we must learn to see through their eyes and not in-stantly rush to analyze their teachings from our cultural perspective. Having been trained to be critical and judgmental and led to believe that our knowledge was the "right" knowledge, it may take some time just to open up and listen without judgment.

๑๑

I am so blessed by this wisdom. I offer what I have learned to those who are ready to hear.

CLOSING POEM

◄○►◄○►◄○►◄○►◄○►◄○►◄○►◄○►◄○►◄○►◄○►◄○►◄○►◄○►◄○►◄○►

OH WOMAN OF THE MIST!

—Woman Who Sits on the Rock

Her heart aches for her children and their children's children.

She has always known her roots and connection are a central part
and one with Mother Earth.

Her spirit hurts and screams as "The Master" rips her womb apart
and says "You are to listen to 'The Man.' You are a part of
'The Man.' God made you from his rib."

What garbage! What rubbish!

Her elders—her Grandmothers and their Grandmothers raised her
as the centre and being of the people. They told her, "You
are the core, the backbone of our people."

Her Father and his Father's Father told her she was holy, sacred,
and without her, the people could not go on. They honoured her and made her feel special. They did this through
teaching the young men the importance of all of life. They
showed the young men how to offer tobacco and give
thanks for life—to be humble and grateful for the life
givers.

© Woman Who Sits on the Rock (Lenore Stiffarm), 1993.

POSTSCRIPT

◄◦►◄◦►◄◦►◄◦►◄◦►◄◦►◄◦►◄◦►◄◦►◄◦►◄◦►◄◦►◄◦►◄◦►◄◦►◄◦►◄◦►◄◦►

As I came to the close of writing this book, I found my mind tenderly and longingly wrapping itself around each quote that I had gathered over these last few years. It was especially difficult to choose entries for the last month, as I have more than enough material for at least another book—and more waiting in the wings from planned times with Maori, American Indian, Hawaiian, and Australian Aboriginal Elders in the near future.

Being with the people quoted in this book, reading the writings of Native people, and then sifting through the many quotes collected has been an ongoing and deeply moving spiritual experience. This process has provided me with a daily soaking in a global spiritual bath. My spirit lingers with this wisdom, like lovers who, when parting, slowly pull away from each other until only the very tips of their fingers still caress.

I know that I will never leave this material and this wisdom, yet this kind of deep daily support for my spirituality may get "lost in the shuffle" if I let it. I hope not to. These daily readings will be mine, too, and I will use them as well as other material I have, for new ideas, other writing, and time with the Native people who are my interconnected *whanau*.

I hope in some small way that sitting with this book has enriched and broadened your life, offered new information and healing, and opened new doors. If so, the book has served its purpose.

I feel honored to have had the love and support and the guidance of Elders to write it, and I hope my learnings reflect their teachings. This book feels like doing the work of the Creator, and doing the work of the Creator is the most joyful work there is. I am grateful for the opportunity.

The most important contribution that Phil Lane, Sr., wanted to give to this book is an old, old saying: *"Wakan-Tanka kokipapi pin he wasapa oinkpa kin he e"* (Honoring God is the beginning of wisdom).

May this book honor the Elders and the Native people who have so freely given their wisdom, guidance, and support—And in so doing, honor the Creator.

CREDITS

◄O►◄O►◄O►◄O►◄O►◄O►◄O►◄O►◄O►◄O►◄O►◄O►◄O►◄O►◄O►◄O►◄O►

GRATEFUL ACKNOWLEDGMENT IS MADE TO THE FOLLOWING FOR PERMISSION TO REPRINT MATERIAL:

Alaska Native Language Center, for excerpts from *Athabaskan Biography Series*, University of Alaska, P.O. Box 757680, Fairbanks, AK 99775.

Latifa Amdur, N.D., L. Ac., Dipl. Ac. and C.H., for entries dated January 20, April 6, July 15, December 3, and December 11.

Michael Annesley, The Celtic Aboriginal Foundation, P.O. Box 286, Cronulla, NSW 2230, Australia, for permission to reprint from *Burnum Burnum's Aboriginal Australia: A Traveller's Guide*, Burnum Burnum.

Andrea Axtell, for entries dated November 29 and December 8.

Horace Axtell, for entries dated August 18 and November 19.

Bear & Co., Inc., for excerpts from *Medicine Cards*, by Jamie Sams and David Carson, Copyright 1988, Bear & Co., Inc., P.O. Box 2860, Santa Fe, NM 87504.

Bishop Museum Press, Bernice Pauahi Bishop Museum, Honolulu, Hawaii, for excerpts from *Ka Po'e Kahiko: The People of Old*, Samuel Manaiakalani Kamakau.

'Ros Bowden and Bill Bunbury, for excerpts from *Being Aboriginal: Comments, observations and stories from Aboriginal Australians*, Australian Broadcasting Corporation Books, copyright Australian Broadcasting Corporation, 1990.

Eddie Box, Sr., for entries dated November 3 and December 3.

The Center for Action and Contemplation, P.O. Box 12464, Albuquerque, NM 87195-2464, for "A Hopi Warning," Thomas Banyacya, interviewed by Richard Rohr, OFM, originally printed in *Radical Grace*, used with permission.

Ann Kondo Corum, for excerpts from *Folk Wisdom of Hawai'i: or don't take bananas on a boat*, by Ann Kondo Corum, used with permission of the author.

Council Oak Publishing, Inc., 1350 E. Fifteenth St., Tulsa, OK 74120, for permission to reprint from *A Cherokee Feast of Days*, © 1992 by Joyce Sequichie Hifler.

Don Coyhis, President, White Bison, 6755 Earl Dr., Colorado Springs, CO 80918, for entry dated January 3.

Vine Deloria, Jr., for entry dated September 11.

Derek Fowell and Cambridge University Press, 40 W. 20th St., New York, NY 10011-4211, for permission to reprint from *Living Aboriginal Histories: Stories in the Oral Tradition*, Alick Jackomos and Derek Fowell.

George Goodstriker, for entries dated February 1, April 12, May 5, June 25, September 4, and September 25.

Hui Hanai, an Auxiliary of the Queen Lili'uokalani Children's Center, 1300 Halona St., Honolulu, HI 96817, for permission to reprint from *Nana I Ke Kumu (Look to the Source)*, Vols. 1 & 2, Mary Kawena Pukui, E.W. Haertig, M.D., Catherine A. Lee.

David Hancock, Hancock Publishers, 1431 Harrison Ave., Blaine, WA 98230.

Jennifer Isaacs and Lansdowne Publishing, for excerpts from *Australian Dreaming: 40,000 Years of Aboriginal History*, Jennifer Isaacs, editor, Lansdowne Publishing Pty Ltd, Sydney NSW, Australia, © 1984.

Lupita Johnson and *Winds of Change:*, "Living in Canyon de Chelly," reprinted with permission of the author, from *Winds of Change* magazine – American Indian Education & Opportunity,

Winter, 1992; Volume 7, Number 1 • ISSN #0888-8612, published by the American Indian Science & Engineering Society (AISES), 1630 30th St., Suite 301, Boulder, CO 80301 • (303) 939-0023 © All rights reserved.

Franklin Kahn, for entries dated April 26 and November 11.

Maggie Kavanaugh, "Minyma Tjuta Tjunguringkula Kunpuringanyi: Women Growing Strong Together," Ngaanyatjarra Pitjantjatjara Yankunytjatjara, Women's Council Aboriginal Corporation, P.O. Box 2189, Alice Springs, NT 0871.

Reuben Kelly, for entries dated April 23, June 10, September 24, and November 15.

Phil Lane, Jr., Four Worlds Development Project, University of Lethbridge, 4401 University Dr., Lethbridge, Alberta T1K 3M4, Canada.

Phil Lane, Sr., for entries dated February 26, April 8, May 24, July 25, August 24, October 7, and December 10.

Angeline Locey, for entry dated January 24.

Cluny and La'avasa Macpherson, for excerpts from *Samoan Medical Belief and Practice*, with permission of Cluny Macpherson, D.Phil.

Magabala Books, Western Australia, © 1989, for permission to reprint from *Story About Feeling*, Bill Neidjie.

Thomas E. Mails, *Fools Crow*, University of Nebraska Press, Lincoln, NE, first Bison Book printing, with permission of the author.

Henrietta Mann, for entry dated November 22.

Leinani Melville and The Theosophical Publishing House, for excerpts from *Children of the Rainbow: The religion, legends and gods of pre-Christian Hawaii*, The Theosophical Publishing House, P.O. Box 270, Wheaton, IL 60189.

Mercier Press, for excerpts from *Islanders*, Peader O'Donnell, The Mercier Press, 5 French St., Cork, Ireland.

Ms. Magazine, © 1990, for permission to reprint from "Papua New Guinea and the 'Aquatic Continent' " by Margaret Taylor.

New World Library, San Rafael, CA 94903, for permission to reprint from *Native American Wisdom*, by Kent Nerburn and Louise Menglekoch, © 1991.

Helena Norberg-Hodge, for excerpts from *Ancient Futures*, International Soc. for Ecology & Culture, The Ladakh Project, P.O. Box 9475, Berkeley, CA 94709.

The O'Brien Press, Ltd., 20 Victoria Road, Rathgar, Dublin 6, Ireland, for permission to reprint from *Irish Wit: Religion, the Law, Literature, Love, Drink, Wisdom and Proverbs*, Sean McCann.

Pacific Way, 178 Hargreaves St., College Hill, Private Bag 92512, Wellesley St., Auckland, New Zealand, for permission to reprint from "New Zealander Mira Szaszy," Mira Szaszy.

Al Qöyawayma, for entries dated May 18 and July 29.

Rangimare (Rose) Pere, for excerpts from *te wheke: A Celebration of Infinite Wisdom*, and *Kaituhi*, with permission of the author.

Reed Publishing Ltd., for excerpts from *Tangi and Whanau*, Witi Ihimaera, Heinemann Reed Publishers, 39 Rawene Road, Private Bag 34901, Birkenhead, Auckland 10, New Zealand.

Miria Simpson & Daphne Brasell Assoc. Press, for permission to reprint from Dame Te Atairangikaahu, from *He Rourou Iti*, 306 Tinakori Road, P.O. Box 12 214, Thorndon, Wellington, New Zealand.

Colin Smythe Ltd, Buckinghamshire, England, © 1977, for permission to reprint from *The Fairy-Faith in Celtic Countries*, by W. Y. Evans Wentz.

Lenore Stiffarm, for entry dated March 29.

Theytus Books Ltd., for excerpts originally printed in *The Native Creative Process*, by Douglas Cardinal and Jeannette Armstrong, published by Theytus Books Ltd., P.O. Box 20040, Penticton, B.C. V2A 8K3, Canada.

Jeanette Timentwa, for entries dated June 24 and December 12.

Victoria University Press, for excerpts from *Talking Health but Doing Sickness: Studies in Samoan Health*, Patricia Kinloch, editor, Victoria University Press, Wellington, New Zealand, © Patricia Kinloch, 1985.

Albert Wendt and Longman Paul Ltd., Private Bag 102908, North Shore Mail Centre, Glenfield, Auckland 10, New Zealand, for excerpts from *Sons of the Return Home*.

417

SUBJECT INDEX

◄◊►◄◊►◄◊►◄◊►◄◊►◄◊►◄◊►◄◊►◄◊►◄◊►◄◊►◄◊►◄◊►◄◊►◄◊►◄◊►◄◊►

420

ABOUT THE AUTHOR

Anne Wilson Schaef, Ph.D., in addition to
being a world-renowned lecturer and orga-
nizational consultant, is also president of
Wilson Schaef Associates, Inc. She is the author of numerous books which have been
translated worldwide. She lives in Montana
and Hawaii.

OTHER BOOKS BY ANNE WILSON SCHAEF:

The Addictive Organization

Beyond Therapy, Beyond Science:
A New Model for Healing the Whole Person

Co-Dependence:
Misunderstood, Mistreated

Laugh! I Thought I'd Die (If I Didn't):
Meditations and Healing Through Humor

Meditations for Women Who Do Too Much

When Society Becomes an Addict

Women's Reality:
*An Emerging Female System in a
White Male Society*

Praise for Anne Wilson Schaef and
Native Wisdom for White Minds

"When I pass a molehill, I say to myself: 'Down there is another who shows off his centric view of the world!' What an ingenious way Anne Wilson Schaef has found in *Native Wisdom for White Minds* to take us out in the daylight of universal human wisdom!"

—Everlyn Nicodemus
Painter and writer
Born in Kilimanjaro, Tanzania

"In my being I 'know' this book! The very printing of the words brings me closer to 'being' what the essence of living means to me, as a recovering addict, recovering human being, recovering Maori warrior. To just be, at one with all the Creator has given, and to carry that message in being . . . I sense this book has been shared with me, and many others—our *whanau*—and I am warmed to the culmination of and gathering of this information."

—Ihaia Briggs
Maori
New Zealand

"Anne Wilson Schaef has been a friend to Native People for many years. Her writings are incredibly insightful. Many times, I think she's ten years ahead of her time. Her travels to homes of indigenous people all over the world allow her to have special insights that very few human beings have. The teachings of the Elders in this meditation book will help heal many people."

—Don Coyhis
Mohican Nation